Christian Faith

Christian Faith

A Brief Introduction

Peter C. Hodgson

Westminster John Knox Press
LOUISVILLE
LONDON·LEIDEN

Book design by Sharon Adams
Cover design by Kathy York

First edition
Published by Westminster John Knox Press
Louisville, Kentucky

This book is printed on acid-free paper that meets the American National Standards Institute Z39.48 standard. ∞

PRINTED IN THE UNITED STATES OF AMERICA

01 02 03 04 05 06 07 08 09 10 — 10 9 8 7 6 5 4 3 2 1

Library of Congress Cataloging-in-Publication Data

Hodgson, Peter Crafts, 1934–
    Christian faith : a brief introduction/Peter C. Hodgson.—1st ed.
        p. cm.
    Includes bibliographical references and index.
    ISBN 0-664-22417-2 (pbk. : alk. paper)
    1. Theology, Doctrinal. I. Title.

BT65 .H63 2001
230—dc21   2001017787

Contents

Preface

This brief introduction is intended for beginning students of theology. Several new Christian theologies have appeared in recent years, but only a few are well suited for introductory purposes. My own work, *Winds of the Spirit: A Constructive Christian Theology* (Westminster John Knox Press, 1994), though based on lectures developed for foundational courses in theology, is more than an introduction: it is a mini-systematic theology. In the present book, the basic ideas of *Winds of the Spirit* have been reworked, and new ideas have been introduced, all in much briefer scope.

What I offer is not a survey of Christian doctrines in their classical and modern formulations but rather a reflective essay in which I attempt to think about the central Christian themes in relation to three sets of issues that confront humankind with increasing urgency at the beginning of the third millennium: ecological and cosmological awareness, the struggle for justice, and cultural and religious pluralism. These issues not only pose tough questions to Christian faith but also provide surprising resources for a revisioning of this faith. I invite readers to participate in a thought project that engages in both questioning and revisioning. Thus, although the work is introductory, it is not easy in the sense of providing simple answers. The topic demands the best thinking that author and readers alike can bring to bear.

Following an introductory chapter that sets forth the challenges of a new millennium, I focus on five main themes: theology as a way of thinking, God and the world, human nature and evil, Jesus Christ and redemption, and the coming of the Holy Spirit. These themes are central to any interpretation of Christian faith, and the way that I organize them follows a rather traditional trinitarian order, which is explained at the end of chapter 2. But the challenges posed to these themes by today's cultural context require a fundamental rethinking of them.

The book has (with one exception) no notes. Instead, in the bibliography, I indicate some of the major resources on which I have relied in thinking about Christian theology, and I also give suggestions for further reading. These works are mostly modern and recent, and scant justice is done to the rich historical legacy of theology. Several introductory works and theological dictionaries are listed for chapter 2, and those marked by asterisks would be good references for further study. In the glossary, I provide definitions of a number of key theological terms. If in doubt about the meaning of a word, check the glossary.

I have included exercises at the end of each chapter. They are intended to help readers engage in the process of thinking theologically on their own. My assumption is that persons of faith (or those seeking faith) already have many potential theological resources and insights, and that these can be elicited through an imaginative pedagogy. The exercises merely illustrate what can be done in a classroom or in a church study group. I encourage teachers to use and modify them in ways appropriate to their own settings. The exercises are also useful for independent study. They provide a way of reviewing, challenging, and thinking further about the ideas discussed in each of the chapters.

Paul DeHart, Sallie McFague, and Richard Quinn read the manuscript and offered helpful suggestions for improving it. The exercises reflect something of what I learned from two teaching assistants in a class taught at Vanderbilt Divinity School: Charlene Burns and Ellen Ott Marshall. Stephanie Egnotovich has been a wise and firm editor. My thanks goes to all of them.

Peter C. Hodgson

1

A New Millennium:
Whence Courage, Whither Faith?

Challenges of a New Millennium

I am writing and you are reading this book shortly after a special moment in human history, one that, since the time of Christ, occurred only once before: the transition to a new millennium, the third of the common era. People seem to approach millennial time frames and transitions with great anxiety and expectation. Early Christians believed that Christ would return to earth and reign for a thousand years, either very soon or after a thousand-year reign of demonic forces. Some Christians still expect a literal return of Christ or an apocalyptic destruction of the world, but the more common millennial anxiety associated with the present transition was the so-called Y2K problem connected with the year 2000 (the end of the second millennium) rather than with 2001 (the beginning of the third). Computers made the transition to the year 2000 with much less difficulty than expected, but what about human beings? What will the human journey be like during the next century, to say nothing of the next thousand years?

We can scarcely imagine ourselves living in 1001 or 3001. A thousand years ago, Europe was still undergoing consolidation. Various hordes of "barbarians" assailed Western Christendom in the ninth century but were gradually assimilated into the Christian empire, and frontiers began to be pushed back. The Vikings briefly touched

America in 1000; in 1001, Saint Stephen was crowned as the first
Christian king of the Magyars, and thereby established the kingdom
of Hungary, which lasted, astonishingly, until 1918. At the same time,
West and East were drifting apart, and the schism between the
Roman Catholic and the Greek Orthodox Churches became official
in 1054. Thus the entity that we know as Europe was coming into
existence. It was not very impressive by comparison with the more
refined and advanced cultures of Byzantium, India, and China, but a
remarkable period of growth shortly began, ushering in the European
civilization of the High Middle Ages. There was as yet virtually no
contact with other parts of the world—with much of Asia and Africa
and all of the Americas. Living conditions were primitive, but we can
assume that people made love, tilled crops, raised children, and
enjoyed festivals.

The changes in human consciousness and in the human condition
between 1001 and 2001 seem enormous, and indeed they are. Given
the ever-accelerating rate of change, especially during the past two
centuries, the differences between 2001 and 3001 are likely to be
much greater. Because we are limited by time and experience, we cannot begin to imagine what life will be like a thousand years from now.
Will people still love one another, raise crops and children, and gather
for parties? Or will they live only in virtual reality? In view of the
enormous risks that lie ahead, there may not be a 3001 as far as human
history is concerned. One is not inclined to feel overly confident
while pondering this millennial shift, and Christians must acknowledge that the future of Christianity is as uncertain as the future of
humanity as a whole.

It helps to remind ourselves of the arbitrariness of round numbers
and of measuring time in days, years, decades, centuries, and millennia—the strange result of combining an astronomical rhythm (the
earth's rotation on its axis and its revolution around the sun) with an
Arabic numerical system (which goes from one to zero and counts in
tens). Equally arbitrary, and more than a little presumptuous, is the
reckoning of time from the birth of a particular religious figure, Jesus
Christ. The arbitrariness is reinforced by the fact that if the common
era really counted time from the birth of Christ the third millennium
would have begun between 1993 and 1997 because the birth probably
occurred between 8 and 4 B.C.E. Moreover, the world insisted on

celebrating the new millennium in the year 2000, which was actually
the last year of the second millennium; it was the numerical rollover
from 1999 to 2000 that fascinated us. Still, this arbitrary combination
of circumstances has produced the lived experience of time in which
we humans (especially in the West) find ourselves immersed, and it is
pointless to try to extricate ourselves from it. Even our scientific cal-
culations and our machines are dependent on it, and a more abstract
or logical system would serve little useful purpose. The best that can
be said is that a temporal transition such as the one we are going
through provides an occasion for taking stock, for thinking retrospec-
tively and prospectively, and it is good that we should do so.

For practical purposes, we can limit our reflections to the beginning
of the third millennium, to what might happen during the next few
years or decades. Even so, the challenges are awesome, for the twentieth century—the "Christian century," which was also the most violent in human history—has bequeathed staggering problems that
demand immediate and sustained attention. These problems are critical, but they are not simply negative: they contain the germ of new
and even transformative possibilities. The three challenges that I have
in mind are (1) *ecological and cosmological awareness*, (2) *the struggle for
justice*, and (3) *cultural and religious pluralism*. They define the context
for theological reflection on Christian faith today, and I attempt to
show how they help to establish our approach to the central themes of
this faith, namely, God, humanity, Christ, and Spirit. The meaning of
God for today must be sought against the background of ecological
and cosmological awareness; the meaning of humanity against that of
the struggle for justice; the meaning of Christ against that of cultural
and religious pluralism; and the meaning of Spirit in the context of all
three of these challenges, which come together, perhaps, to form a new
spirituality. I do not mean to suggest that these challenges are new. In
one sense, they are old and perennial problems that every *culture* faced,
but the form in which they present themselves today is new.

Ecological and Cosmological Awareness

Human beings have always been aware that they are part of the natural world. Indeed, before the beginnings of modern science in the
seventeenth century and the introduction of mechanical models for

understanding how the cosmos works, humans saw themselves as inti-
mately connected with the natural rhythms and forces of their environment. The earliest religions were religions of nature, which
located the divine power in natural entities such as the sun, the moon,
mountains, rivers, water, wind, fire; or in living beings such as animals, ancestors, and specially endowed persons. Even as divinity came
to be differentiated from these forms, it remained closely connected
to them, as the abundant nature imagery of the Hebrew Bible makes
clear. Civilizations developed as people learned how to use the forces
of nature to their own advantage by means such as hunting and gathering, agriculture, the building of shelters in which to live and to hold
public activities, and the use of material elements to express artistic
and intellectual creativity (carvings, paintings, written alphabets,
music). Nature was a mysterious and overwhelming force, which
could wipe out feeble human achievements through storms and dis-
eases, and its vastness made travels beyond people's local environments difficult and often hazardous. Humans were basically at the
mercy of the natural world in which they lived.

The postmodern ecological movement is partly an attempt to
recover and reactivate this premodern cosmological awareness, but
under vastly changed conditions. Although in the strict sense the word
ecology means the study of the relations between living organisms and
their environments, in a broader and less technical sense it indicates the
interdependence of all the living and nonliving systems of the earth,
indeed of the cosmos. The point of ecology is that everything is internally connected in a delicate web of living and nonliving systems. The
ecological model is not a mechanical model but an organic, relational
model, and it is based on a quantum physics that understands nature in
terms of relations of energy rather than of bits of matter (atoms or substances). Entities do not exist before relations, but *are* modes of relating. The natural world is an extraordinarily complex dynamic system,
in which everything is fluid and interactive, with indeterminacy at the
microlevel and unpredictability at the macrolevel. The old dualisms
between matter and spirit, body and soul, determinacy and freedom,
order and creativity, break down; and new possibilities for understanding the interaction of God and the world present themselves. I explore
some of these possibilities in chapter 3.

The principal change that has occurred during the period of *moder-*

nity is that human beings have gained power over nature and are no longer so much at its mercy. This statement is only relatively true, of course, because natural disasters occur with regularity, and large populations are still ravaged by disease and hunger. Yet nature is now understood on a scientific basis, and understanding brings knowledge, control, and power. With the enhancement of instruments of control, human actions threaten the natural environment as never before.

Two kinds of threats have become especially obvious today: first, the ravages of the environment caused by the pollution of air, water, and soil, depletion of natural resources, and destruction of habitats and species, and second, uncontrolled population growth. Because of the delicate balance of natural forces and their interlocking character, the environment is highly fragile, and only a few degrees' increase in ocean temperatures, possibly caused by global warming from greenhouse gases, brings new and often destructive weather patterns and melting of polar ice. These changes happen gradually and often imperceptibly, so that effective political action to combat them is very difficult to organize. Ecology takes a backseat to other political and economic agendas, especially when it requires any sacrifice in comfort, convenience, and profitability. Indeed, environmental policy has become the latest target of right-wing politics, something to be stigmatized along with feminism, homosexuality, and socialism. This may be a classic instance of a situation where irreversible damage must occur before public consciousness is sufficiently aroused to take corrective action. History affords many examples of such cases.

The uncontrolled growth in world population began about two centuries ago and is increasing at an exponential rate. The growth is linked partly to improvements in medical treatment and food production, but it is driven by other socioeconomic factors such as lack of education, ideological opposition to birth control and abortion, and political or territorial ambition. Technology and politics have conspired to create an extremely dangerous situation, likely to lead to ethnic conflicts, wars, widespread poverty, and mass starvation. The quality of human life is being sacrificed to quantity, and environmental ravages are intensified. Parts of Africa have been deforested for the sake of cultivation and gathering wood for fuel and shelter, but deforestation in turn leads to drought, soil erosion, and crop failure. Increased use of the internal combustion engine in densely populated parts of Asia could result in air pollution far worse than anything yet experienced.

Beyond these immediate challenges is a growing awareness that humanity will not survive forever. Conditions on earth and in our solar system will eventually make human life unsustainable: the greenhouse effect, a new ice age, a pronounced shift in weather patterns, the impact of asteroids, solar radiation, or solar burnout. The period of human civilization on our planet may prove to be a brief epoch in the history of the cosmos, and with that awareness comes a sense of the catastrophic and a recognition of the extraordinary fragility of life. To save us from despair, we need something more compelling in being and value than the indefinite prolongation of humanity. Investing our hopes in scientific ingenuity provides only a false security. We are certainly not the first generation of humans to face the catastrophic—witness the spread of bubonic plague across Europe in the late Middle Ages—but the scale seems vaster now and the results more irreversible, even if remote from our personal lives.

The Quest for Justice

The quest for justice is as old as the human condition itself, and accompanying this condition is a tragic proclivity toward injustice and evil, as I examine in chapter 4. The story of the origins of humanity in the Book of Genesis does not progress far before it is told that Adam and Eve rebelled against the divine command and that one of their sons, Cain, killed his brother Abel in a fit of jealousy. This primeval murder was the archetype of injustice, and before long the corruption and violence it engendered had spread to the ends of the earth. The situation became so desperate that God determined to destroy the human race and to save only a righteous remnant. All these events occur in the first ten chapters of Genesis. The flood provided only a temporary respite in the history of injustice: the rest of the Bible bears witness to this reality.

What is new about the human condition at the beginning of the third millennium of the common era? The change is principally one of the enhancement of human power through technological mastery of the forces of nature—the same change that has produced the environmental crisis. Perhaps Cain killed Abel with an ax or a stone, but today's efficient killing machines can destroy dozens, hundreds, thousands, or even millions with the pull of a trigger or switch. Economic power has become concentrated in the hands of corporate elites who exercise enormous influence over the lives of people across the globe. These elites are driven not by ideals of justice and solidarity but by motives of profit and market share. The goals of democracy are corrupted by money, information management, and deceptive advertising. Many inhumane practices of the past have been eliminated, but in their place has emerged a culture in which violence has become a form of entertainment—unrestrained, gratuitous, and digitally enhanced to the point that suffering loses all redemptive significance. The Internet provides recipes for making bombs and websites for hate groups. Human beings are not more wicked now, but the instruments of wickedness are vastly improved—out of proportion, it seems, to the instruments of goodness.

Yet there remains a great hunger for justice. The Victorian novelist George Eliot* suggested in one of her stories that justice is like the kingdom of God: it is not without us as a fact at which someone can point and say, "There it is"; rather it is within us as a great yearning. Justice is first a utopian-religious ideal rather than a legal-political reality. Yet having the vision of justice within us as a great yearning motivates us to engage in practices that make this world a tolerable, perhaps a better, place in which to live. The utopian vision can inspire an infusion of justice into political and social policy. Having such a vision and yearning implies a faith that the ultimate cosmic mystery (the God of the kingdom) is a power of justice rather than of injustice.

The *liberation movements and theologies* of our time—feminist, black, womanist, gay and lesbian, Hispanic, Latin American, Asian, African—bear witness to this insight: an awakening of consciousness,

---

George Eliot is the pen name for Mary Ann (or Marian) Evans (1819–1880), who wrote some of the finest works of fiction in the English language. Religious themes and figures appear in all her novels, and her ideas are, in my view, of interest in theological efforts to rethink the nature of religious faith in our own time. Her work is a neglected nineteenth-century resource, which I have attempted to recover in a recently published book, *Theology in the Fiction of George Eliot: The Mystery beneath the Real* (London: SCM Press; Minneapolis: Fortress Press, 2001).

a glimpse of the kingdom of justice, an unwillingness to tolerate conditions of oppression any longer—these are the first steps in bringing about a change in objective conditions. Seeing that things could be different is necessary for the struggle to make them different. Heightened consciousness, such as that evoked by the sexual and gender revolutions, not only envisions new possibilities but also uncovers a labyrinthine system of repressions and oppressions concealed beneath the surface practices of the dominant culture.

Thus the liberation movements raise the stakes: evil proves to be a more complex, subtle, intractable reality than earlier generations had imagined, and justice seems to be a more elusive goal. The stakes are raised also by the terrifying power of the instruments of destruction that humanity has devised. The next global conflict could well be the last. Time is running out for the discovery of an alternative to war and violent resolution of conflicts. This new situation at the beginning of the third millennium poses a formidable challenge in that force continues to be necessary to restrain criminals and tyrants, to say nothing of greedy human beings in positions of power.

What is the alternative? What are justice, peace, love, reconciliation, solidarity? How are they accomplished in the face of human depravity? These terms resist easy definition, and we need a paradigm of these ideals and their accompanying practices as we confront the challenges of the twenty-first century. The great religious traditions offer such paradigms, and we must draw on the wisdom they offer. For Christians, the paradigm focuses on Jesus Christ and the new way of being in the world that he envisioned with the metaphor of God's kingdom, which is above all a kingdom of justice—a realm of right, true, gracious, and mutually enhancing relationships among human beings and in the cosmos. Justice has ecological implications—indeed is a form of ecology—and it is linked to the first of the challenges we have identified. Moreover, there are many visions of justice, of which the Christian is only one. How can we adjudicate the differences in these visions and make them productive?

Cultural and Religious Pluralism

One of the great facts of human existence is that others also exist and impinge on our lives in various ways—others who are like us as well as others who are not like us. The latter used to be stigmatized as pagans or barbarians, and systematic efforts were undertaken to remove, destroy, or convert them. Such practices continue to the present under the euphemism of "ethnic cleansing." Fear and hatred of the other have a powerful grip on the human psyche because of the insecurities that threaten our own existence. These insecurities have been heightened in modern times as a result of the increasing communication and interaction among once-isolated cultures. It is ironic but not surprising that just as the human species seems to be moving toward a truly global community, fanaticism in the advocacy of party, people, creed, culture, or region has also intensified. Differences cannot be assimilated into a common culture; they must be allowed to stand in their rich and threatening diversity. Moving to a stance of genuine pluralism, in which a diversity of beliefs and practices is freely acknowledged and valued, is not easy to accomplish intellectually and emotionally, for it requires the abandonment of cherished absolutes and comforting certainties. Many people cannot make such a transition and so resort to a defensive stance.

Is the alternative to absolutism a debilitating intellectual and ethical relativism, the loss of any persuasive sense of truth, value, goodness, beauty? This option is also widespread: the cultured elite, as opposed to the popular masses, favors it. This view leads to cynicism, *nihilism*, aestheticism, a tendency to play with truths as though they were toys, presuming that everything is subjective and arbitrary, a product of this or that creative fantasy. Yet with the loss of truth come lies and deception; with the loss of value, self-interest; with the loss of goodness, power for the sake of power; with the loss of beauty, entertainment and consumption. Relativism has social and political as well as philosophical implications.

Is there a third way, an alternative to the options of fanaticism versus relativism, fundamentalism versus secularism, uncritical dogma versus an absence of any conviction? The eroding middle ground of a critical or reflective religious faith is part of the new situation that confronts us at the beginning of the third millennium. The concrete way that I propose to address this challenge is in the form of the question raised in chapter 5: Who and where is Christ for us today? Can one affirm loyalty to Jesus as the Christ in the context of a diversity of great religious traditions, each with unique insight into truth and value, each possessing rough moral and intellectual equivalence? Perhaps loyalty to Christ provides a way of opening ourselves to redemptive transformation wherever and however it appears. Thus, far from demanding an exclusivist posture or presuming that all other religious figures are included in and under Christ, a critical faith in Christ may provide a theological basis for religious pluralism. This at least is the possibility I explore, together with an exploration of questions of justice and injustice in relation to a theology of human being and an exploration of ecological and cosmological awareness in relation to a theology of God and the world. In this way, I hope to weave the challenges of a new millennium into a reformulation of the central themes of Christian theology.

Whence Courage?

The challenges confronting the new millennium seem overwhelming. Is it realistic to presume that governments and corporations will act quickly and decisively enough to avert a major environmental disaster? Even if they do, is the human species not doomed to ultimate extinction? Given the unbroken history of violence and injustice that have accompanied civilization from the beginning, can we have any confidence that in the third millennium things will be different? If they are not different, what will prevent the use of nuclear, biological, and chemical weapons of mass destruction? Even if the major powers are united in the determination to ban the use of such weapons, totalitarian states, fanatic tyrants, and terrorists will pose a continuing threat. Once the knowledge of how to make weapons becomes available, it cannot be withdrawn or canceled; only the means of production can be restricted. Constant vigilance is required, but it is not foolproof. Finally, in light of the parochialism, *ethnocentrism*, and *xenophobia* that have characterized most of human history, can we expect that a genuinely global culture will emerge in the future, one in which differences are honored and protected while cooperation, sharing, and interaction are maximized? There are hopeful signs in this direction, but at the same time resurgent nationalisms are replacing the dominance of superpowers, and regional conflicts are multiplying. Even if cultures do manage to dwell together peacefully, will it be possible to affirm the relative truth and validity of one's own *tradition* while acknowledging the validity of others? What will prevent the erosion of moral and religious traditions and their replacement by an amorphous cynicism and *hedonism*—the negative products of cultural relativism?

Under such circumstances, we must ask how and where people find the courage to be, think, live, and act. Again, this is not a new question, for courage has been a requisite of existence for as long as human beings have been around. Courage was one of the classical moral virtues along with prudence, justice, and piety, but the circumstances under which the question is raised have changed, become more urgent. At the beginning of the twentieth century, the German theologian Ernst Troeltsch had this sense. He wondered whether human beings could muster the courage to rebuild after the most devastating war of history, which seemed to presage the end of Western civilization. His answer was that we must simply take the risk of acting on the best premises available in ambiguous circumstances, not knowing the outcome with certainty. A pragmatic approach is more effective than a theoretical attempt to answer all questions in advance. We must have the courage to take the first step, to try things out. The American *pragmatists* William James and John Dewey offered a similar answer.

What gives us the strength to take that step when we seem to be at the end of our rope, when the odds are against us, when we experience pain and discouragement? George Eliot wrote to one of her friends that the highest calling of human beings is to do without opium and to live through all our pain with conscious, clear-eyed endurance. It is so easy to become depressed, passive, cynical, dependent on pain relievers and narcotics; or conversely, to become hyperactive, manic, driven. To say that it is our "highest calling" to learn how to endure in a conscious, intentional way, to conquer pain rather than to escape it, is to hint that this is an ethical responsibility with a religious aspect. Religious faith can indeed provide strength; it can be an enduring resource rather than a momentary respite. Yet it is also tempting to find in religion an escape, a false consolation which promises future reward in the form of life after death.

Thus George Eliot sought a religion that would enable persons to do without consolation and that would refocus responsibility on human needs here and now. Similarly, the French philosopher and

Reformed theologian Paul Ricoeur called for a religious faith beyond both accusation and consolation, beyond the threat of divine punishment or the promise of divine reward. He believed that a certain resignation or consent is required: we must learn to accept what is given and not attempt to change what cannot be changed, but we can hope for the better and work to achieve it. We must not lose the confidence that it *is* possible to act and to make a difference, taking one step at a time, without a clear understanding of how we fit into the overall scheme of things or of how we can solve the momentous problems of our time. Many little steps are required, many unhistoric acts, many hidden lives lived faithfully: they will make a difference. If we are ready to give up our illusions, fears, ambitions, and self-centeredness, we may experience something like the grace of courage. It comes in a mysterious way, but from where?

Whither Faith?

A certain faith emerges when human *beings* find the courage to think, live, and act. Courage both solicits faith and requires *faith*. Without faith, humanity is condemned to a hell of meaninglessness, of alternation between pleasure seeking and death seeking. Life becomes a tale full of sound and fury, signifying nothing. For most Western peoples, religious faith today has become tangential to the central activities of their lives. It is something optional, an add-on, a leisure activity, not the core motivation for living and acting. In ancient cultures, such as those of Israel and Greece, as well as in medieval and early modern Europe, religion was the integrating substance, infusing and binding everything together into a structure of meaningfulness. People lived in a religiously significant world—a world that was in many ways oppressive and superstitious, but purposeful and oriented to clear ends. The last three centuries of the second millennium attacked oppression and superstition in the name of reason and science, accomplishing in the process the secularization of consciousness and the ghettoization of religion.

Will this trend continue into the third millennium, or will a reversal occur? Without a reversal, it is difficult to see how people will find the resources to live meaningfully and courageously, but an enduring reversal cannot be a reversion to premodern forms of consciousness, which would force us to live in two disconnected worlds, the world of religion and the world of science. The challenge rather is to work through the insights of science and to incorporate them into a new form of religious faith, one that coheres with a scientific vision of the cosmos, affirms the struggle for justice heightened by the liberation movements, and shares in the cultural pluralism of *postmodernity*.

The "whither" of faith is the same as the "whence" of courage—namely, God, the Ultimate *Mystery* of the cosmos, the beginning and end of all things. Can we affirm this belief at the beginning of the third millennium? Can we believe in a divine reality that transcends the world as its alpha and omega while being immanent in the world as the power by which everything is? Can we believe that the ultimate cosmic mystery works for justice rather than injustice, despite the tragic nature of the human condition, and that it manifests itself in a diversity of religious traditions and cultural forms, none of which can claim exclusive and privileged insight, but each of which has its own validity and makes a distinctive contribution to an inexhaustible whole?

Such a faith is capable of sustaining the courage to face the daunting tasks of the twenty-first century. Insofar as such courage and faith actually appear in the world today, they bear witness to the reality of that which calls them forth, their ultimate whence and whither. They are not self-generating but a response to something that presents itself. People of moral courage and religious faith have a sense of being confronted with something that is overwhelmingly real and important. There is no other proof of God. We cannot explain how such courage and faith come about, but we can rejoice in their presence and pray for their strengthening. We know only that we ourselves—finite, fallible, faulty beings that we are—cannot be their source.

Themes and Questions: A Revisionary Approach

In the following chapters, I address five central themes of Christian faith: theology as a way of thinking, God and the world, human nature and evil, Jesus Christ and redemption, the coming of the Holy Spirit. I do not simply repeat these traditional themes but attempt to revise them in light of questions and challenges at the dawn of a new millennium.

1. Is theology an intellectually credible activity any longer? What calls it forth and legitimates it? What are its ways of thinking, its relation to faith and revelation, its resources, dimensions, and structure? Is theology simply an exercise of human *imagination*, or does it respond to something real that comes forth in redemptive transformations, something awesome and overwhelming, yet gracious and sustaining?

2. Is it appropriate to think of God and the world as interacting, and if so is God in some sense affected by the world? What happens to the traditional affirmation of divine *immutability* and sovereignty? Is it possible to combine faith in God with a postmodern cosmological and ecological consciousness? Is the doctrine of the Trinity a clue to the God-world interaction, or is it an anachronistic remnant of a mythological and patriarchal form of religion?

3. What is the relationship of human beings to nature and to God? How can we humans be both embodied beings and free spirits? Is the human condition a tragic one? Is sin a necessary byproduct of being finite and free? If so, what does this imply about the goodness and power of God? Can any theology take account of radical evil, which serves no redemptive purpose? Is the quest for justice fruitless?

4. Who and where is Jesus Christ for today? Is Christ singular or plural, divine or human, or both? How does the redemption wrought by Christ actually work in the everyday world? How do Christians express their loyalty to Christ while acknowledging the validity of other faiths?

5. Is it an impossible dream to think of the third millennium as the age of the Spirit? What is *Spirit?* Is there a spirituality for today that might actually contribute to the building of a commonwealth of justice? Can religion ever get beyond accusation and consolation? What does it mean to place one's ultimate hope in God the Spirit?

By addressing these questions to these themes, I assume that it is possible and necessary to reconstruct or revision Christian faith in ever-changing circumstances. Such revisionings have gone on for two thousand years, and they make Christianity a living religion as opposed to a museum piece. The reconstructions of the past now seem to us part of well-established tradition, but in their own context they were often regarded as radical and disruptive. Indeed, theological controversies became life-and-death matters, and people suffered for their convictions.

It seems strange today to hear people say that such revisionings are impossible or dishonest—that we must either adhere to traditional creeds and formulas or renounce the religion of the Bible and Christian orthodoxy. People who say this want either to hold onto the traditional forms uncompromisingly or to abandon religious faith entirely. They assume a fundamental incompatibility between the culture of Christian belief and the culture of the modern secular world. They try to make a liberal, revisionist form of theology look weak and accommodating. Yet the greatest theologians have avoided the extremes of Christ versus culture. For the most part, they have sought a mediation, knowing that Christ challenges every cultural form, but also that such forms are the necessary vehicle of a reflective faith. Think of Origen and Augustine, Anselm and Thomas Aquinas, Luther and Calvin, Schleiermacher and Hegel, Troeltsch and Barth, Tillich and the Niebuhrs, feminist and liberation theologians.

Some might want to categorize my approach as a revisionary *theology of correlation* in the tradition of Paul Tillich and Protestant liberalism. I do not quarrel with this way of locating me on the spectrum of theological options today, which run from *fundamentalism* and *radical orthodoxy* through *postliberalism* and revisionary *liberalism* to *deconstruction* and *agnosticism* or *atheism*. I think the best theology is done toward the center of this spectrum, but basically I am not interested in such categorizations, which tend to caricature positions other than our own. I believe we benefit from a diversity of theological efforts and should not attempt to constrain them. Most important, I am convinced that theological revisioning is an effort any serious Christian can engage in. I invite you to try it as you read this book.

EXERCISES

1. Here is a simple true-false quiz. Before reading the next chapters, answer the following questions as true (T) or false (F). Share your results with other members of the class or group, and discuss their significance. Keep a record of your answers, and after finishing the book take the quiz again to find out whether your mind has changed on any of these questions, or whether the reasons for the answers you give have changed.

    a. Theology is a language game.

    b. Faith is a necessary condition for thinking theologically.

    c. God is not dependent on the world to be God.

    d. Faith must be subjected to critical reflection.

    e. Theology is a systematic exposition of unchanging truths.

    f. Cultural context is a factor of equal importance with scripture and tradition in determining the meaning of Christian faith.

    g. It is possible to maintain faith in Jesus Christ while affirming the truth and validity of other world religions.

    h. Sin is a necessary condition of being human.

    i. History has a purpose and direction.

    j. The beginning of the third millennium offers the possibility of a spiritual renewal.

2. Take a few minutes to write down your reflections on the significance or insignificance of the beginning of the third millennium, thoughts you had at the time of the millennial transition or things that occur to you now. Share your reflections with the person sitting next to you and then with the whole class.

3. Divide the class into three groups. Each group will focus on one of the challenges identified in this chapter: ecological and cosmological awareness, the quest for justice, and cultural and religious pluralism. What are the negative as well as positive features—the threats as well as the resources—in each challenge? How do the challenges relate to one another? Is one of them more critical or basic than the others? Come back together with reports from each of the groups, followed by general discussion.

4. What do *you* regard as the characteristic features of the postmodern world in which we live—features that challenge religious faith or provide resources for rethinking it? In particular, which aspects of postmodernity have been left out of account in this book?

5. Is it appropriate to rethink what Christians believe about God, the world, humanity, sin and evil, Jesus Christ, and the Holy Spirit in light of constantly changing cultural situations? Would such rethinking diminish the authority of scripture and tradition? Form two teams to debate this question.

6. We live in a largely secular culture in which moral values such as courage, loyalty, prudence, and justice are often affirmed and

practiced without having any religious faith, that is, without belief in an ultimate source and criterion of values that transcends all human capacities. Are morality and religion separable or inseparable? In class, write down on a blackboard (or on a sheet of paper if you are working individually) arguments in support of both sides of this question, and assess them; or form an electronic chat group on this topic.

7. Whence courage, whither faith?

2

Thinking Theologically: What Calls It Forth?

Faith, Revelation, and Theology

The brief answer to this chapter's question is that faith calls forth *theology*. Theology participates in a movement toward understanding already implicit in faith, a movement that Anselm of Canterbury referred to as *fides quarens intellectum*, "faith seeking understanding." Why should faith seek understanding, and what calls forth faith in the first place?

Faith seeks understanding because *faith itself is a kind of thinking, knowing, or reasoning*. It is not an antirational activity but a distinctive kind of reasoning, which has at least two aspects. On one hand, *faith is an immediate, participatory apprehension of truth* and has the character of feeling, emotion, intuition. It is affective rather than reflective, practical rather than theoretical. Such knowledge comes from direct experience and involves all of our receptive capacities. Feeling and emotion are more prominent than is critical judgment. In the stance of faith, we feel that we are part of something that appropriates us, something that we accept as constituting the reality of the world in which we live, something from which we derive a basic confidence or certainty. This feeling is a kind of knowing, but faith seeks further understanding of its content. It is impelled by its inner nature to thematize the felt, intuited reality, to bring it to speech in figurative language, to make it an object of reflection, to communicate it.

We see this happening in biblical texts. In the Bible, faith is rational and discursive, an articulation deriving from certain fundamental ways of experiencing God's presence in the world.

On the other hand, faith is a knowledge mediated by trustworthy persons, texts, scriptures, testimonies, communities. Faith is holding something to be true on the ground of trust in another—say, a physician whose expertise we trust or witnesses to an event that we do not see ourselves. The fabric of human society is made up of such trusting knowledge, and we are in trouble if the fabric begins to break down. Trust is necessary because the range of personal knowledge is limited (I do not know much about how computers work) and because, practically speaking, it is impossible to verify the assumptions involved in every action (when I proceed on a green traffic light, I assume that a red light shines for the cross street and that other drivers will obey it). We must act on assumptions that we cannot test every time. H. Richard Niebuhr observed that the major part of our intellectual furniture consists of faith in this sense; it is the indispensable basis of daily life. Thus Christian faith is part of a larger nexus of trust: it is the holding-as-true of the testimonies that make up the Christian tradition.

Why should we trust our immediate apprehensions? What renders the mediators of knowledge trustworthy? Ultimately, it is the trustworthiness of the truth that comes to us in these two ways. Trustworthiness is the only thing that elicits trust, and what we call "revelation" is the manifestation of the trustworthiness of ultimate reality. Thus another crucial aspect of faith is that it is a knowing *founded on and oriented to a revelatory experience that grasps and shapes it.* Faith is a knowing that finds itself at the disposal of what is known; it encounters a disclosure that it cannot manipulate or control but that it learns to trust. The self is cognitively active in the stance of faith, but what it knows is a gratuity that shapes, empowers, and defines *it* rather than vice versa. This experience of encountering something ultimate in being, truth, and value, *which discloses itself in and through our very act of knowing and trusting it,* lies at the heart of all authentic religious faith.

Theology is called forth by faith, but faith is called forth by revelation. What is revelation? This question is one of the most difficult and misunderstood in all of theology. The root sense of the word in

English, Latin, and Greek is that of drawing back (*re*) a veil (*velum*) or covering. *Revelation* means an unveiling, an unconcealment, a disclosure of what is hidden. Implicit in this double negative (un-veiling) is the hint that the veil remains present even as it is drawn back. In the case of God, at least, the hiddenness and mystery of what is revealed are not destroyed; indeed, what is revealed about ultimate reality is precisely its hiddenness and mystery, without which it would not be ultimate.

Thus, as Martin Luther, Karl Barth, and Paul Tillich emphasized, divine revelation has a paradoxical character: It entails veiling as well as unveiling; God remains hidden even as God is revealed. This idea expresses another paradox, namely, that God is a *mystery*—a rational mystery. A mystery is not something irrational; rather it contains a higher rationality, a higher truth, which we cannot know by means of ordinary categories or speak about directly. In the Greek mystery cults, such truth was communicated by oracles, and in their presence people kept kept their eyes closed and mouths shut (*myein*). We are mute in the presence of mystery. This attitude is the origin of *mysticism* and *negative theology*, but negative theology presupposes and facilitates *positive theology*, a theology of revelation.

It is a mistake to think of revelation as laying bare the divine nature, perhaps in the form of truths or propositions that tell us what God is. Yet most of us tend to think of revelation in this way. It is difficult to escape the notion of revelation as God's transmission of information about divine things in *supernatural* form, but revelation is not a set of truths from another world. It is an event of unconcealment—of opening, healing, communication, *redemption*—in this world, in the process of which God is disclosed *indirectly*. The unveiling that occurs in revelation refers directly to the world and only indirectly to God. God is not the direct object of disclosure; rather God makes godself known or communicates godself in and through the events by which the *world* is unconcealed (opened, healed, emancipated) as the One who speaks and therefore *is* the primordial Word that opens beings, redeems reason, liberates persons and structures.

The association of God, God's Spirit, with wind, breath, word, and light in the Hebrew Bible is of great significance. These media of divine power and presence are fluid and intangible. The wind that blows, the light that lightens, the word that discloses remain the *means* of revelation. They do not become the object of revelation. We cannot see the divine wind, look into the divine light, or speak the divine word; in the presence of God, we must close our eyes and shut our mouths. To see God, we must look at the world and what happens in it; to speak about God, we must engage in worldly words and deeds. We do not see wind but rather what it moves; we do not listen to breath but to the words it forms; we do not look *at* light but see *by* it. If we attempt to fix our gaze on the luminous source of light, we are blinded; light itself we see only as reflected by illumined objects.

In the process of revelation, the only thing we learn directly about God is that God is a primordial and everlasting *revelatoriness*—not the object of revelation but the *event* or *power* of revelation itself. The intrinsic characteristic of God is to be open, manifest, revelatory, not hidden, withdrawn, locked up in godself. The divine hiddenness or veiling is a condition of possibility for unveiling, not the other way around. The unveiling occurs indirectly, through the world. The world veils God. Yet God comes forth, enters into the world, brings about redemptive transformations by the revelatory power that we symbolize as wind, word, light. Revelatory-redemptive power itself remains an inexhaustible mystery.

A close connection exists between revelation and redemption. In chapter 5 I ask how God works redemptively in history—what the focus and character of this work are, and how this work transpires as a historical process. The revelatory character of God's redemptive work calls forth faith and legitimates faith and theology. Yet we can know and articulate this activity of God as true redemption and thus also as valid revelation only by faith and theology. A circular relation exists among redemption, revelation, faith, and theology. Theology is called forth and verified by that which it interprets as valid and trustworthy. All knowledge is ultimately circular, and it is folly to think that we can escape the circle of interpretation, but we must learn to come into the circle in the right way and to work through it as rigorously as possible.

The word *theology* simply means language or thought (*logos*) about God (*theos*). This etymology tells us that the ultimate subject matter of theology is God, and if theology is to be true to its name, it cannot rest content with any subject other than this one, despite its elusiveness, intangibility, and deep mystery. The task of theology, David Kelsey tells us, is to seek to understand God more truly, but as we have seen, it is impossible to know or to speak about God directly. Thus we must turn to the proximate subject matter of theology, which is language—the language of faith, which is called forth by God's self-revelation in the world. In theology, we usually do not talk directly about God but about faith's language about God. The language of faith is the place where God's self-revelation and self-presentation take place. Language about God is here intended in a very broad sense to include worship, practices, texts, traditions, theological systems, ethical judgments, works of art, bodily performances, music, and ultimately silence in the presence of the holy. These modes of communication constitute God-related matters, and in seeking to understand God, theology turns principally to them.

The language of faith in this rich sense is irreducibly symbolic, *imaginative*, metaphorical, embedded in texts, stories, traditions, practices. It is necessarily so because it attempts to bring to speech what we cannot directly express. At the same time, this language always presses toward thoughts, concepts, doctrines. The symbols themselves give rise to thought, as Paul Ricoeur remarked in a trenchant formulation. The heart has its reasons, said Pascal; faith seeks understanding, claimed Anselm. Faith seeks meaning and truth, and claims about meaning and truth involve analysis, clarification, judgment, publicly available discourse.

Here theology comes into play. The *logos* of *theos-logos* means not simply "word" or "language" but also "logic," "reason," "thought." We must *think* about faith's language about God, and theology proper does not begin until thinking occurs. The thinking of theology incorporates the *metaphors* of faith, but it seeks to work out concepts or doctrines by which specific metaphorical insights are brought together into a more comprehensive frame of reference. In this way, the metaphors are not forgotten but reflectively illuminated. By thinking about faith's language about God, we strive to understand more fully what it means to say that God is both a mighty whirlwind of history and a still small voice of conscience, or that Jesus Christ is both the incarnate Word of God and a sensuous human being, or that by becoming incarnate in a human nature God does not divinize that nature but deepens its finitude. In this way, apparently contradictory insights are woven into a fabric of understanding with rich contrasts and a unifying pattern.

Ways of Thinking Theologically

All knowledge, I have suggested, is circular, and the process of interpretation is circular. Sometimes this process of interpretation is referred to as the "hermeneutical circle." Hermes was the messenger of the gods, who interpreted the gods to humans and communicated between gods and humans; *hermeneutics* simply means the science or principles of interpretation.

One way of understanding the hermeneutical circle is to suggest that a circulation occurs among three principal elements in the interpretative process: the *root experiences* of human life in the world, which are events in which a revelation or disclosure of ultimate being and meaning occurs; the *expressions* of the root experiences in the texts and traditions that constitute the stream of culture; and the *situation* of those who interpret the root experiences mediated by texts and other cultural expressions. There is something that lies in front of a text, a fore-text, as well as a text and a con-text—a message to which the text points as well as a source (the text itself) and a situation.

The status of what is before the text—that to which it refers—is intangible in the sense that we never have access to it directly but only as it comes forth in the process of interpreting texts. Yet it is important to insist on the reality of what is before the text, for otherwise we are left only with interpreters and texts (which themselves are interpretations) and no reference to truth, no subject matter of interpretation, nothing about which the texts make claims and interpreters make judgments—nothing, that is, other than interpreters themselves, and interpretation becomes purely subjective. The struggle against subjectivism and relativism is one of the challenges of postmodernity, but the alternative is not an objectivism that diminishes the role of the interpreter or identifies ultimate truth (the *Word of God*) with the textual media (the words of scripture). What lies before the text must be distinguished from the text even as it is mediated by the text through acts of interpretation.

The three elements of the hermeneutical circle are connected by two movements or ways of thinking. The first, *critical-explanatory thinking*, entails a backward, questioning movement from the inter-preter through the textual media to the root or revelatory experience, which is established as an object of critical scrutiny. This movement is thinking in the form of science, *scientia*, which is disciplined, methodical, theory-based knowledge. It requires the interpreter's ini-tiative whereby a range of experience is analyzed, taken apart, and set up before the mind as an object of investigation. It involves a flow of meaning from the interpreter through the medium to the experience, but then, in the case of *root* experiences, a strange thing happens. A *reversal* in the flow of meaning occurs, so that revelatory experience now discloses itself on its own terms and by its own power, through its own primary symbols, rather than by having a constructed mean-ing imposed on it.

This process gives rise to the second way of thinking, *practical-appropriative thinking*, which entails a forward, answering move-ment from the root experience through the textual media to the interpreter, a movement to which we as interpreters belong and in which we experience something like a disclosure. We both appropriate this movement, make it our own, and are appropri-ated by it, caught up in it. This is a movement of participatory practice, by which we shape the world in which we live, and from which we derive the pre-understandings that are the fundamental source of the concepts that make critical thinking possible. This is thinking in the form of *paideia*, the ancient Greek term for the formation of character through the acquisition of practical wis-dom. Wherever we enter the hermeneutical circle, whether at the point of critical theory or of participatory practice, we are in the middle of things; something is always presupposed, something always follows, and we must work our way through the circuit in disciplined fashion.

As an example of how the circuit works, we can start with a the-ory of revelation, such as the one offered earlier in this chapter. Rev-elation means taking back a veil, an unconcealing, and we look at examples of how human beings disclose themselves to one another through words and deeds. We apply this notion to God and think that God is revealed by divine words and deeds in history, but then we encounter a shaking event that transforms our lives. We come to realize that God is not simply laid open and explained by such events—that God is not an object like other objects in our experience. We begin to see that God is the subject, not the object of revelation, that God's very being is intrinsically revelatory—the power of revelation that can work redemptively in our lives if we respond to it, letting it shine on our fears and hopes, pretensions and desires. Our lives can be transformed by this illumination. We are led in turn to a richer conception of revelation, and the whole process is understood a bit more clearly.

Theological thinking shares in the lack of secure foundations that is characteristic of this circular model. There is no absolute starting point, no bedrock of certainty, not in the root experiences or scripture and tradition or the personal experience of believers or interpreters. These elements become truly revelatory of ultimate reality only when they work together, when they are brought into hermeneutical play through the back-and-forth movement of thinking. Revelation is not a fixed deposit of truth but occurs through a process of interpretation by which elements are related to one another in always-changing circumstances.

We might think of theology as a ship that floats and sails in a fluid medium when its component parts work together well—its hull, mast, sail, rudder, fittings. Nothing external to the ship props it up mechanically. It functions by means of a symbiotic relation with its environment—water and air. Purposes are achieved, such as tacking into the wind or sailing to a destination, through an interactive process. This sailing image is an apt one in the age of postmodernity for understanding how truth occurs. It is appropriate to an ecological model of the cosmos and to a pluralistic understanding of culture. It acknowledges the relativity of truth claims but does not abandon the quest for truth. It avoids both a hopeless relativism and a rigid absolutism. Truth occurs in terms of mutually interdependent relations. Everything is related, and thus everything is a matter of interpretation. Criteria of truth and judgments about truth develop principally through consensus, both the consensus represented by well-established and influential traditions and the consensus that forms anew through conversation, debate, and persuasion.

The two ways of thinking theologically—critical-explanatory and practical-appropriative—help to specify how theology is related to faith yet is distinct from faith. As practical-appropriative thinking, theology participates in the act of faith itself and in the experience that gives rise to faith, namely, revelation. It participates in the event of appropriation. Rather than simply making revelation an object of critical scrutiny, theology engages in the thinking called forth by the revelation of God; it is a thinking rigorously controlled by and directed to its ultimate subject matter, God. But theology also engages in critical-explanatory thinking, which means that its participation in the practice of faith must be of a special sort. It is more like the historian's empathetic participation in the life of a figure of the historical past than it is an immediate act of faith itself. *Empathy* means participation from without; thus the theologian who is also a believer must learn to disengage him- or herself from faith as a confessional act to participate in it as a theologian. Theology requires a critical distancing from the shared experience as well as an empathetic appropriation of it. The insider must become an outsider, and the outsider an insider.

The second way of thinking, critical-explanatory, brings theology into proximity with the scientific study of religion or what is generally referred to today as religious studies. Again there is a difference: religious studies places primary emphasis on critical analysis and comparative description, and it is reluctant to identify itself with a faith perspective. Theology attempts to live in two worlds and to mediate between them—the world of scientific analysis and the world of paideutic practice. These worlds need each other even as they threaten to pull apart from each other. The scientific observer's critical analysis needs a life-enriching engagement with the materials of religion to avoid becoming a deadly historicism. The believer's confessional involvement needs the critical scrutiny of the scholar of religion to avoid becoming a dogmatic acceptance of whatever traditional authorities claim. Perhaps the best way of describing the theologian's stance is as one of *critical engagement*. Theology is at once a theoretical and a practical discipline. It seeks wisdom and truth as well as scientific explanation. Because there is an inherent tension between these elements, theology is not entirely welcome in either the church or the university. Theology seeks to make the tension a productive one for both of the worlds in which it lives.

The Resources and Dimensions of Theology

Resources

Resources are the tools that theology uses in the thinking process. They provide the content or material for critically and practically reflecting on faith's language about God. The resources of theology include scriptures, traditions, cultures, and experience. All of these resources are media of a redemptive-revelatory reality with which they can never be identified; but without them no access to redemption is available. The resources are necessary bearers of something that always transcends them, of something that comes to pass in the process of thinking about them and of acting on their basis.

1. *Scriptures.* For Christian theology, the Bible is the basic resource because it is the original document that bears witness to the revelatory events on which Christian faith is based and to which it refers. Frequently the Bible has been *identified* with these revelatory events and has been endowed with the supernatural qualities of infallibility, inerrancy, inspiration, and—as the unique deposit of revelation—unchallengeable authority. Similar qualities have often been extended to the teaching authority of the church or to theological tradition. Such claims on behalf of scripture and tradition have been severely tested and largely discredited during the past two centuries, despite the fact that many people continue to hold them. These documents are clearly human products, sharing the insights and limitations of the cultures that produced them.

For Christian faith, the paradigmatic figure of Jesus of Nazareth is the decisive nucleus of the transition to redemptive existence. The precise meaning of redemptive existence and the way that Jesus is the agent of it are discussed in chapter 5. Jesus' story had to assume linguistic embodiment if it was to be efficacious for subsequent generations. This occurred first, orally, in the apostolic witness, but then expanded to a body of writings whose function was to contribute to the upbuilding of the community of faith. These writings came to be called the New Testament and had the character principally of *kerygma*, proclamation, witness to Jesus as the Christ. In this way, they were distinguished from the Hebrew Bible, whose primary genre was that of *torah* or instruction, as well as from the Christian *dogma* or *doctrine* that came later. What makes the New Testament writings of central importance for Christians is not their official *canonical* status, but the character of the writings themselves as bearing a unique witness to the originative event and as containing intrinsic literary and theological power to evoke a fresh disclosure of God and consequent redemptive transformations of human existence. Writings having these qualities came to be regarded as scripture in the Christian community, just as other literatures have become classics for the wider human community.

The writings of Israel are also an essential vehicle of redemption because the faith of Israel is immanent in and constitutive of Christianity as well as of Judaism. The gospel proclaimed by Jesus presupposed the faith of Israel and radicalized it, made it universally available. The literature of Israel, Hebrew Scripture, is a much richer resource for many of the central themes of faith—God, creation, providence, idolatry, sin, wisdom, worship, justice—than is the literature of the New Testament. The latter on its own cannot function as an adequate scripture for a religious community.

Referring to the two literatures as Old Testament and New Testament can reflect the assumption that the old covenant of God with the people of Israel has been superseded by a new and superior covenant. This unfortunate assumption has contributed to a long history of persecution and prejudice. Although Christianity is *different* from Judaism, it is not *better* than Judaism. The differences focus on the way that Christians view the figure of Jesus and the work of redemption, but Christians cannot claim that their religion is superior to other religions because they have Jesus. Such an attitude is inappropriate in an age of religious pluralism, and indeed the differences between Judaism and Christianity should be understood according to a pluralistic rather than a hierarchical model. The situation is complicated by the fact that the Hebrew Bible functions as sacred scripture for both religions.

We should not view such an approach to the authority of scripture as detracting from its revelatory power. Revelation occurs *in* and *through* processes of redemptive transformation. Because the Bible is the essential written vehicle of redemption for Jews and Christians, it is a profoundly revelatory document. Indeed, it is God's self-revelation because it is precisely God's redemptive activity in history and in the hearts of believers that evoked the writing of scripture in the first place and that fuels its ongoing *interpretation*. God's self-revelation, however, is not limited to scripture.

2. *Traditions.* In addition to the Hebrew Bible and the New Testament, there is the subsequent interpretative tradition. Communities are shaped not only by events of origin but also by controversies, crises, and interpretations that make up their ongoing tradition. *Tradition (traditio)* means to deliver or hand over what has been given, but every handing over is an interpretation in which something new is added as well. This is necessary because over time the content of tradition becomes settled or sedimented, and it needs to be stirred up by fresh interpretative efforts, which reflect new controversies, questions, and insights. Each new generation must interpret anew what has been given to it because its situation is different. There is no one standard theology that will last forever; theology must be rewritten by each generation and from ever-changing perspectives. Older theologies become valued classics from which we continue to draw resources, but they are no longer a living interpretation of Christian faith. We in our own time and place are responsible for the living interpretations.

There are not one but many streams of interpretation—a mainstream or dominant stream and many subordinate and often marginalized streams. This fact should not surprise us if tradition is formed from the controversies, conflicts, and crises of living interpretation. History is usually written by the victors, who have a tendency to suppress their opponents and erase any memories of them. The marginalized or heretical traditions—such as spiritual, mystical, and utopian sects, the writings of women and of freethinkers—have however displayed a remarkable ability to survive and can be recovered through diligent research.

Western theology has not only suppressed deviant elements within its own history but has also ignored the presence of Christianity in other cultures, partly through ignorance and partly on the assumption of superiority. A wealth of Christian traditions abounds both in the European–North American stream and outside it—in Asia, Australia, Africa, Central and South America; in Greek and Russian Orthodoxy; in many forms of Catholicism and Protestantism. As we shift to a multicultural perspective, the study of theology becomes much richer and also more complicated. Most of us must acknowledge our limited knowledge and must keep ourselves open to an ever-widening world.

We live in a religiously plural world. Christianity, with all its internal diversity, is only one of the religious faiths of humankind. Other great and ancient traditions stand alongside Christianity, each internally diverse as well: Judaism, Islam, Hinduism, Buddhism, Confucianism, Taoism, the primal religions of Asia, Africa, and the Americas. Unprejudiced knowledge of these other traditions has become widely available only in the past century, and Christians are learning that these traditions can also be an important resource for their own theological reflection, and can contribute to the very *substance* of Christian theology. In the new millennium, it will be as important for a Christian to know in some depth at least one other religion and to be committed to inter-religious dialogue as it is to know her or his own tradition and scriptures. In fact, we do not really know our own tradition without knowing others. Our own faith will be enormously enriched, deepened, and extended through dialogue with other religions, and through dialogue the religions will not remain the same.

The goal is not a fusion of traditions into an amorphous world faith, but the discovery of points of similarity where the insights of others can strengthen our own, and also the discovery of points of difference where the illuminating alternatives and rich possibilities of human spirituality can be appreciated. Competition and conflict among religions ought to be a thing of the past, for religious intolerance has bred some of the most dreadful wars of history. With the stakes heightened for peace or global annihilation in the new millennium and with the prospect of a totally secularized world in which people look to technology for meaning and hope, religions must make common cause on behalf of peace and the revitalizing of spiritual resources. Precisely where this will lead Christian faith and theology in the future no one knows, but we must have courage to embark on the journey. Abandoning the old posture of superiority and exclusivity, and opening ourselves to a cooperative sharing with other traditions, does not mean abandoning our deep commitment to the gospel of Jesus Christ.

3. *Cultures.* Religions are deeply embedded in the cultures that produced them and to which they contribute resources. Paul Tillich remarked that religion is the substance of culture, and culture the

form of religion. Thus religious traditions cannot be studied in abstraction, and the history and interpretation of culture is another important resource for theology. Religious themes of great significance are implicit in philosophies, political systems and ideologies, artistic styles and works of art, fiction and poetry, ethical and social principles, professional practices, popular culture—all the things that make up the social matrix in which religion occurs. Much of the best theology being done today is interdisciplinary, involving philosophy, history, literary criticism, social theory, anthropology, and cultural studies. In this book, I draw the themes I have identified as special challenges—ecological and cosmological awareness, the struggle for justice, and cultural and religious pluralism—from reflection on the cultural situation at the beginning of a new millennium. In this way, I introduce cultural resources into the heart of the theological project. Theology must take a cautious stance in relation to culture, appreciating its creative power but remaining wary of its demonic potential, its tendency toward idolatry. Unfortunately the creative and the demonic are sometimes closely connected.

The cultural context from which a particular theology emerges establishes its social location and shapes it to a degree greater than has generally been acknowledged. No theology is neutral. It arises with a particular set of questions shaped by the situation in which it finds itself. Questions establish the content of theology as much as do answers. Whoever determines the questions also determines the answers to a considerable extent. Analyses of the role of social location in constructing reality have underscored this point, as have African American, liberation, and feminist theologies. The latter have helped us appreciate that the questions by which the tradition is interpreted always reflect particular interests and ideological biases. Generally it has been the theological and ecclesiastical mainstream, the "establishment," that has determined these questions, rather than oppressed and marginalized groups. Yet it is precisely the questions that have arisen from the situation of these groups that have brought to light new meanings hidden in ancient texts as well as aspects of human experience and existence that have not been thought about before. New streams of interpretation and experience—Asian and African, Latin American, African American, Hispanic, feminist, gay and lesbian—are flowing alongside the Western mainstream.

4. *Experience.* The final resource on which theology draws is experience. *Experience* is a very broad and rich term. It can refer to the root, revelatory experiences from which religious faiths arise and draw sustenance. These are generally events of a social character to which a community bears witness, such as the exodus of Israel from Egypt, or the conveyance of God's commandments to the people of Israel at Mount Sinai, or the figure of Jesus around whom disciples gathered and from whom a new community emerged, or the creation of Protestant Christianity through the reforms of Luther and Calvin.

The term can also refer to the distinctive experiences of a confessional, national, ethnic, or sexual group, such as "the Catholic experience," "the American experience," "the black experience," "women's experience," or "the gay experience." Cultural, historical, psychological, and emotional elements shape these group identities and the theologies that flow from them.

Finally, and most commonly, the term designates personal experience. The lives of mystics, great religious autobiographies, and classic psychological studies such as those of William James show how important a resource religious experience is; liberation theologies point to the necessary role of *spirituality*, of personal religious experience, in a life of committed practice. Authentic spirituality—life in and through the power of the Spirit—is at the very heart of Christian faith. No theology can be sustained without such experience.

Experience is the great teacher, the means by which the Holy Spirit teaches us. It entails an internalizing, a making our own, of the rich resources provided by scripture, tradition, and culture. Without these other resources, it is empty; without it, the others are a dead content. The resources must work together to be effective; they must be brought into a hermeneutically productive relation. The church accomplishes this through its liturgy, preaching, educational programs, pastoral care, and social mission. Theology accomplishes it through the interplay of the dimensions into which its work is divided.

Dimensions

The theology that accompanies Christian faith is a large and complex undertaking. It is impossible to accomplish all of its tasks with a single effort. The situation has become more demanding as tradition accumulates, the range of knowledge expands, and the methods of interpreting a subject matter multiply. The beginnings of specialization can be traced to the medieval universities, yet still in the nineteenth century a single professor could cover several of the theological disciplines. But no longer. Theology, like other departments of academic study today, has become preoccupied with disciplinary specialization, and it has been all too ready to sacrifice breadth of vision to highly compartmentalized technical competence.

Although they have increasingly functioned as autonomous disciplines, I prefer to think of the subdivisions of theological study as dimensions of a shared whole. That whole is theology in the sense of a critical engagement with faith's language about God. This is the common subject matter of a theological school or a university department of theology, although the whole is rarely referred to as "theology" any more. The three major dimensions I identify are *historical theology*, *practical theology*, and *constructive theology*. They are unified by sharing in the task common to theology, that of understanding God more truly, and they are distinguished by the elements and resources on which each focuses in the circle of interpretation.

1. *Historical Theology: Scripture, Tradition, Religions, Culture.* *Historical theology* deals with the texts, traditions, and other cultural media by which the language of faith has been given expression in the past (up to and including the recent past): the Hebrew and Christian scriptures, the history of the church, the various streams of Christian tradition, the history of other religions, and the history and practices of cultures.

Obviously, what I have named critical-explanatory thinking prevails in the work of historical theology, but not to the exclusion of practical-appropriative thinking. The very purpose of the critical analysis and interpretation of texts is to enable the experience to which those texts bore witness to become alive and meaningful for us today, and this is accomplished by constructing distinctive narrative accounts of what has happened. Thus historical theology, like all historical study, has an inherently practical and ethical dimension. It is also based in one way or another on a worldview, a religious commitment, a theological construal of the meaning and purpose of reality, which for the most part remain implicit and unarticulated.

The term *historical* leaves something to be desired as a name for this first dimension of theology. The critical tools that theologians use to study texts and contexts are by no means solely historical. Sociology, psychology, linguistic and structural analysis, literary criticism, and cultural studies have grown in importance and in some respects are predominant today, especially in biblical studies. Perhaps what makes them historical in a broad sense is their recognition of the narrative structure of texts as well as of the temporality and relativity of contexts. These disciplines exhibit a historical mentality even when their analytical tools are not historical.

2. *Practical Theology: Ecclesiology, Personal Experience, Ethics.* In practical theology, the direct concern is with the appropriation, enactment, and practice of the faith grounded in the revelatory events to which the texts bear witness. As such, the practical-participatory mode of thinking predominates, but not to the exclusion of critical-theoretical thinking. If practice functions apart from theory, it becomes mere technique. Practice provides the pre-understandings, values, and criteria in terms of which critical theories are constructed. At the same time, theological theory is not just a speculative flight of fancy but the foundation of practice in the sense that it offers an interpretation or construction of the events that point to the ultimate source of all practice, God. Theory and practice each support the other, which means that there is no ultimate ground of theological knowledge apart from the spiral of interpretation, the interplay of theory and practice, of critical analysis and practical engagement.

Three broad topics belong to the domain of practical theology: ecclesiology, personal experience, and ethics. Ecclesiology includes an understanding of both the nature of the church and its ministries. Although the nature of the church might be considered a part of constructive theology, it has not belonged among the traditional doctrines, such as God, Christ, creation, sin, redemption, eschatology. We do not believe *in* the church in the same sense that we believe in God or Christ; rather we *are* the church. Ecclesiology is an exercise in self-examination. It has a practical goal, that of actualizing the ecclesial community as a place where redemptive transformations of human existence occur in light of the Christic paradigm and of ministering to the world in and through the church. The church has need of leadership—of leaders whose task is to form, preserve, and nurture the faith and life of the ecclesial community. Specialized ministries are called forth by the specific needs of community formation and preservation. These ministries have traditionally fallen into four groups: proclamation and teaching, worship and sacraments, care and service, governance and order. A major responsibility of practical theology is to develop the theory of the practice of these specialized ministries and to contribute to the education of ministers.

As we have seen, personal religious experience is one of the elements in the circle of interpretation and one of the resources of theology. We cannot engage in the work of theology in abstraction from our experiential location, and personal experience contributes significant material for theological analysis. Practical theology reflects on this experiential locus. It analyzes the psychological and social dynamics of personal experience, and in the form of pastoral theology it attends to the spiritual care of individuals. The vast literature of spirituality also belongs in this domain, for it seeks to nurture personal experience, often by sharing the experiences of especially sensitive individuals. This is the function of the great religious autobiographies from Saint Augustine to Dorothy Day. A good recent example is the writing of Kathleen Norris.

Christian ethics is related to both constructive and practical theology and bridges the two dimensions. It interprets the same symbolic, textual matrix by which faith is expressed as constructive theology does, and it refers to the same root revelatory events. Ethics, however, interprets these matrices and events not in the form of concepts, doctrines, or theological systems, but in the form of principles of action or policies to guide the redemptive practice of faith in social and individual dimensions. In this respect, ethics belongs to practical theology. It draws on the social and psychological sciences for critical tools, and these bring ethics into closer proximity with practical than with constructive theology. Other more philosophical and theological forms of Christian ethics bring it into proximity with constructive theology.

3. *Constructive Theology: The Revelatory Experience of God.* Constructive theology makes the direct object of its concern neither the practice of faith nor the texts of faith but the experience that gives rise to faith—a *revelatory* experience having as its source and reference *God.* Of course, constructive theology has access to this subject matter not directly but only through the root experiences of faith as medi-

ated by the texts of faith. Its purpose is to let the revelatory event come to expression anew, issuing in redemptive transformations of the world in which we live. Thus constructive theology mediates between historical theology and practical theology, drawing on and contributing to both; in it, the critical-explanatory and practical-appropriative modes of thinking attain some balance.

The ultimate subject matter of theology, God, can never come directly into view, can never be grasped or touched. Earlier I suggested that theology is like a ship, a sailing vessel that has no foundation other than itself and is subject to the force of the elements. God is not onboard this ship—but God propels it, draws it forward, is the wind blowing into its sails. On most points of sail, the wind is ahead of the ship, pulling it forward through the vacuum—a negative force—generated on the leeward side of the sails. The ship was an early symbol of the church, which is itself a hermeneutical reality, an event of ongoing interpretation and appropriation.

The ship can also serve as a metaphor for theology, and the relation between wind and ship may help us to understand the relationship between God and theology. God is not an objectifiable, controllable object but blowing, living spiritual power, always ahead of theology, drawing and driving it. Yet without the ship of theology and church, the wind would not be caught; its redemptive power would blow in nature, but not for humans. Wind or breath is the root metaphor present in the word *spirit*, so to think of God as the wind blowing into the sails is to understand God as Spirit—the most unrestricted of the trinitarian *symbols*. Like the wind, the Spirit of God generates a mysterious, attracting-propelling power in the world. God's power is not predominantly that of a positive force. Rather, like a vacuum, God's power is one of negation or emptiness, of powerlessness—which proves to be the greatest power of all.

The Nature of Theological Construction

What I have said thus far about constructive theology distinguishes it from historical and practical theology and metaphorically names its mysterious subject matter. It does not, however, explain what makes it *constructive* or why this adjective may be appropriate, in the age of postmodernity, for describing the formulation of theological concepts and doctrines. Constructive theology has been called by other names in the theological tradition. At one time, it was called *dogmatics* or *dogmatic theology*. Although the Greek word *dogma* means simply the teaching of what is thought to be good, true, and fitting, the dogmas of the church came to be associated with officially sanctioned, authoritative truths that all loyal Christians had to accept. Partly as a consequence, the adjective *dogmatic* acquired a pejorative connotation, meaning "opinionated," "authoritarian," "inflexible." In an age when truth can no longer be understood as a timelessly valid set of propositions, continued use of the word *dogmatic* to name one of the dimensions of theology only confuses matters.

The expression *systematic theology*, popularized by Paul Tillich, is more adequate for our purposes. A *system* (Greek *syn* + *histanai*) is something that is set up or arranged from parts so as to form a unity or organic whole. A theological system is a model, paradigm, or construct that has the purpose of promoting coherence and consistence in thinking about the various thematic components that make up Christian faith, such as God, creation, fall, human nature, sin and evil, Jesus Christ, redemption, the Holy Spirit, the community of faith, eternal life. Are these things just a collection of items, or are they systematically connected with a unifying theme? Tillich pointed out that a system is not necessarily antithetical to the fragmentary and differentiated character of life as it is normally experienced. In each fragment a system is implicit, just as in every part the whole of life is potentially present. A system simply draws out and builds on an experienced fragment of life and vision. We need systems to live and think productively, to avoid waste, error, and repetition; human beings along with other living species are inveterate system builders.

Yet it is easy to get carried away by intellectual systems and to forget their limited, fragmentary, situation-dependent, heuristic character. Here the word *constructive* has certain advantages over *systematic*. Etymologically the words are similar, but the nuances differ slightly. To *construct* means to build things up by putting them together (Latin *com* + *struere*). By a strange quirk, the Latin verb *struere*, "to pile up," comes from an Indo-European root that also means "to scatter," "to spread," or "to strew." To con-strue is to strew things together, to fashion a meaningful arrangement, to bring a semblance of order out of chaos, to make something from straw. The words *strew* and *straw* are etymologically linked: straw is what is strewn about and piled up. Shortly before his death, Thomas Aquinas, the great medieval synthesizer, is said to have remarked, "All that I have written seems like straw to me." He knew that, metaphorically speaking, all that we have to work with in this world is straw ("straw before the wind," in the words of Job), but he also knew that we can and must build things of it.

The work of building, construing, constructing is a basic human work; without it, we cannot dwell humanly in the world. This work also entails a deconstruction—dismantling old structures, using up resources, strewing them differently. To build something new, we must tear down something that humans have already made or destroy something that nature has created. The quantity of physical energy in the universe remains constant, but the usable energy is gradually depleted. Although *entropy* does not apply in the realm of ideas, whenever we critically appropriate what has been thought before, we destroy (de-strue) its original form. This necessity is part of the *paradox* and *tragedy* of human existence. It has become fashionable today to emphasize deconstruction, but those who do so tend to forget that every deconstruction presupposes a construction and that without ever-new attempts at construction human culture would soon disintegrate.

Constructive activity is interpretative activity. To *construct* is to "construe," that is, to explain, deduce the meaning of, interpret. The task of constructive theology is to work out a construal of the meaning and truth of faith's language about God in light of a particular cultural situation. The result is not a finished, permanent, unchanging system; it is an interpretation and nothing but an interpretation. Every attempt to bring coherence into the rich matrix of religious images and experiences, every attempt to move from symbolic to conceptual language is limited and incomplete. To speak of theology as constructive rather than systematic reminds us that theology is a hermeneutical activity, that its construals are made onboard a moving ship. In this sense, theology is like navigation. Navigation enables us to chart and sail the waters with some degree of safety and some sense of direction, but never to control the elemental forces that drive us.

Theology, we must acknowledge, is a project of the human imagination, not a direct description of what things are in and of themselves—whether divine things or worldly things. The question is whether theological constructions are nothing other than illusory fantasies, extensions of the human ego, as Ludwig Feuerbach claimed, or whether they respond to something real, transcendent, and overwhelming that presents itself in experience, demanding reverence, a transition from self-centeredness to reality-centeredness. There is no definitive proof in this matter but only a practical testing of competing reality-construals in terms of their fruits in human life. Does Christian faith lead to a life of authenticity and insight, or are we better served by an agnostic or atheistic way of being in the world? The task of constructive theology is to make the best possible case for the validity and truthfulness of Christian faith, but the risk of faith and the need for courage are never eliminated.

Gordon Kaufman points out that just because the symbol *God* is a product of the human imagination we are not to conclude that God has no reality. All of the symbols by which we live (such as "tree," "I," "world," "light-year") have been created by the human imagination, and this fact does not imply their falsity or emptiness. The question for Kaufman is whether the symbol *God* continues to do the work for which it was created, whether it can continue to function significantly in human life as an ultimate point of reference. If not, it must be reconstructed or dropped.

I share with Kaufman an understanding of theology as a "human imaginative task," but I go about the task of reconstructing the symbol of God differently than he does. The question ultimately, in my view, is not whether the symbol functions effectively, but whether it designates a reality that is true and good in and for itself, a reality that impinges on human consciousness, changes lives, and evokes creative imagination.

There are several ways of organizing the work of constructive theology. One possibility is to identify components or genres such as natural or *foundational theology*, doctrinal or symbolic theology, and apologetic or *philosophical theology*. Another is to identify the actual themes or topics or symbols that together make up the subject matter of Christian faith. These approaches are not incompatible but emphasize different aspects, one procedural, the other thematic. For purposes of this brief introduction, I avoid the complex issues involved in the first approach and focus on the symbols or themes.

Here three problems confront us: Where to start, how to identify the key symbols, and how to relate them.

Should we start with knowledge of ourselves or with knowledge of God? John Calvin posed this question at the beginning of his instruction in the Christian religion. He pointed out that these two forms of knowledge are connected, each presupposing the other, but he concluded that "the order of right teaching" requires that we discuss the knowledge of God first and then proceed to knowledge of ourselves. Kaufman, by contrast, argues that it is better to start with what we are most familiar with, ourselves and our existence in the world, and to move from there to what is lesser known and problematic, namely God and Christ. Many contemporary theologians agree with him, and theological anthropology has become a privileged topic. Kaufman, however, acknowledges that our understanding of the human is modified by our understanding of God and Christ, so that the central Christian categories mutually qualify one another and cannot be simply prioritized.

My own view represents a modification of both Calvin's and Kaufman's views. Where theology actually starts, I think, is with the mystery of faith, from which unfolds the mystery of God's triune self-mediation. I have argued that faith is a knowing that is founded on and oriented to a revelatory experience that grasps and shapes it. Faith is not an autonomous act, an inherent human capacity, but is drawn forth by a power that transcends it. In the mystery of faith, knowledge of self and knowledge of God momentarily fuse, and theology as a way of thinking is called forth. This is what I have attempted to show in this chapter.

The subsequent chapters follow from the way that God becomes manifest in and to the mystery of faith. As is evident from the ancient creeds and liturgical formulas, the structure of the divine self-manifestation for Christians is a *trinitarian* one: God becomes known as Father, Son, and Holy Spirit. From this manifestation derive the several topics of constructive theology and the order of their treatment. Despite many problematic features with the traditional doctrine of the *Trinity*, such as its patriarchal language and mythological conceptuality, it offers deep insight into the nature of God. It brings God into relationship to the world and ourselves, and it makes this relationship constitutive of God in a way that remains to be discussed.

I propose to rethink the triune configuration of God in light of the challenges posed at the beginning of the third millennium, and attempt to show that it accords well with an ecological, emancipatory, and pluralist sensibility. This leads to the specific proposals set forth in chapters 3, 5, 6 (on God, Christ, and Spirit). Chapter 4 locates humanity within the divine economy of creation and redemption and in this respect subordinates knowledge of ourselves to the knowledge of God. The knowledge of God, however, arises from the mystery of faith, and every articulation of this knowledge is a human construction. It is *we* who believe, but *what* we believe is not a projection of ourselves. Our belief is a response to the One who overwhelms us by creative power, comes forth as real for us in redemptive transformations wrought by Christ, and enters into our daily lives and future hopes as Holy Spirit.

The various topics that make up the substance of Christian theology—God, creation, world, humanity, sin and evil, Christ, redemption, Spirit, consummation—derive from the triune mediation of God, the way in which God interacts with godself and with what is not God, the world. This derivation is what makes them properly theological topics and enables theology to be true to its name, the *logos* of *theos*. Such at least is the accumulated wisdom of the Christian tradition with which the project of reconstruction starts and from which it draws continued sustenance. The new insights that we have to offer are modest as compared with this wisdom, but they are worthwhile to the extent that they force *us* to think theologically in relation to our own time and place, not just to repeat what has gone before.

EXERCISES

1. Spend a few minutes writing down your own definition of *faith*. Compare what you have written with the definition of faith provided in this chapter, and note significant differences and further questions. Discuss your results with other members of the class.

2. Form a circle in which each person briefly shares an instance when she or he had an experience of faith or lived by faith. Identify and evaluate common patterns and puzzles as they emerge. What

appear to be the main features of faith experiences? Is it possible for humans to live without any sort of faith whatsoever or, at the other extreme, to live by faith alone?

3. "God is a primordial and everlasting revelatoriness—not the object of revelation but the event or power of revelation itself" (p. 22). Write a brief essay (one or two pages) in which you explain and assess this statement. If you disagree with it, propose a different way of relating "God" and "revelation." Share what you have written in class, or post it in a chat group.

4. Try writing a brief skit or dialogue in which a Jew, a Christian, and a Muslim discuss the distinctive ways that God is "revealed" according to their respective traditions. Some of these might be performed or read before a class.

5. If you are a member of a church or a student in a theological school, ask yourself to what extent the discourses and practices of the church or school are about "God." Ask others what they think, and see what conclusions might be drawn about the presence or absence of "God-talk" in your institution.

6. "Theology is a critical engagement with faith's language about God." Write a page or two in which you reflect on each of the terms in this definition and on the ways they are connected. How would you modify the definition? Exchange your comments with a partner, and discuss what each of you has written.

7. The second section of this chapter (pp. 24–27) offers a model of the "hermeneutical circle" according to which a circulation occurs among three principal elements: root experiences, expression of the experiences in texts and traditions, and the situation of interpreters. The circulation consists of two movements or ways of thinking: critical-explanatory and practical-appropriative. Try to diagram this model on a blackboard, sheet of paper, or computer. Does the picture that emerges look like a line, a circle, an ellipse, or a spiral? What is suggested by these geometric images?

8. How do you react to the following statements in the text? "Revelation is not a fixed deposit of truth but occurs through a process of interpretation by which elements are related to one another in always-changing circumstances." "Everything is related, and thus everything is a matter of interpretation. Criteria of truth and judgments about the truth develop principally through consensus"

(p. 26). These statements are an attempt to find an alternative to both absolutism and relativism. Divide the class into three groups, each representing one of these perspectives on the question of truth: absolutism, relativism, and the mediating position adopted by the text. Formulate arguments for each perspective; then share them in a plenary session.

9. The third section of the chapter (pp. 28–37) suggests that "resources" are the tools that theology makes use of in its critical engagement with faith's language about God. Four such resources are identified: scriptures, traditions, cultures, experience. Divide into four groups. Each group will focus on one of these resources and make the best possible case for it as a necessary tool of theology. Then in a plenary session hear and discuss the arguments for each resource. Keep these questions in mind: Are the resources roughly equal, or should one or more of them be given priority? Do you agree with the idea that the resources work best when they are all brought into play and interact with one another? Are there other resources that have not been mentioned?

10. From a conservative or evangelical Christian perspective, the treatment of scripture in this book is likely to be regarded as inadequate. Why is this the case? If you agree with such a perspective, what changes in a doctrine of scripture are called for? How do you defend the changes? Several different perspectives on scripture might be debated in class, ranging from claims of plenary inspiration and verbal infallibility, through the idea that God makes use of the uses of scripture in the life of a faith community, to the view that scripture is a relative, purely human cultural product.

11. This book uses a metaphor to think about what theology is and how it is related to its ultimate subject matter: theology is a like a ship, a sailing vessel that has no foundation other than itself and is subject to the force of the elements; God is not onboard this ship, but God propels it, draws it forward, is the wind blowing into its sails. Do you find this metaphor helpful or misleading? Why? What are some other metaphors for theology? What are metaphors, and why do humans rely on them?

12. If theology is a construction of the human imagination, as claimed in the fourth section of the chapter (pp. 37–42), what is to prevent us from concluding that the objects of theology are simply pro-

jections of human need or extensions of the human ego? Such a critique of theology was formulated by Ludwig Feuerbach in the nineteenth century. Have a debate among members of a class in which the following positions are represented: (a) the Feuerbachian critique of religion; (b) the view that, although theology is indeed a human construction, it is a response to something real, transcendent, and overwhelming that presents itself in experience; (c) the view that theology is properly based on God's self-revelation in Christ and is not a human construction at all.

13. How would *you* go about constructing a Christian theology? Where would you start, what would be the chief elements or topics, and how would they be related to one another? Let each member of a class or group work up a one-page outline; then share and discuss these with the group as a whole. Look for emergent similarities and contrasts, which may help to identify the main possibilities for doing theology today.

14. What calls forth theology?

3

God and the World:
How Do They Interact?

Any credible concept of God today must be an interactive one. We can no longer think of God as a supreme being who intervenes in the course of world affairs miraculously and at will from somewhere outside the world, controlling events and determining outcomes. Our modern and postmodern worldviews do not allow such a picture, and our personal and corporate experience tells us that it is not so—or, if it is so, that God must be capricious and malevolent. From even a casual glance at ordinary events, it is evident that terrible things happen on a daily basis: innocent persons are slaughtered by fellow human beings, natural disasters strike indiscriminately, people suffer from incurable illnesses, social injustice is tolerated everywhere on earth.

If God were a *transcendent* sovereign being who could prevent such happenings and could assure desired outcomes but did so only occasionally and arbitrarily, then the fact of evil and suffering would be more than enough to falsify belief in such a God. The argument that God provides future compensation for present suffering makes religion into a justification of existing conditions; the argument that God uses destructive means to punish wrongdoing or accomplish some hidden end is a travesty of the very concept of God.

God and the world must be related in a way different from the model of divine sovereignty. The way proposed in this book is an interactive one, in which God and the world affect and influence each other without either determining the other, but also in which the relationship between them is not reduced to one of pure symmetry. As I attempt to show, God and the world affect and influence each other differently, the difference being one between God as *creator* and the world as *creation*. God is not a function of world process but is the creator of world process. The world is not a divine puppet show but a theater of free and independent agents who contribute to the glory and tragedy of the divine life. An interactive approach requires a rethinking of both the world and God in such a way that interactivity and interdependence are introduced into the very nature of each.

In this chapter, this approach takes the form of a relational-organic-ecological view of the world and a creative-trinitarian view of God; it culminates in a portrayal of God-in-the-world and the-world-in-God as Spirit, the consummate figure of the divine life. The perspective that I represent is *cosmotheandric* in the sense intended by Raimundo Panikkar. To Pannikar, *cosmos* (world), *theos* (God), and *anthropos* (humanity) form a complex interactive system whose elements cohere as *pneumatikos* (in and of the Spirit). Humanity is introduced into the system as that aspect of the world in which the world becomes conscious of itself and in which God becomes most fully incarnate, but I defer a discussion of humanity to the next chapter.

A Relational-Organic-Ecological View of the World

For our purposes, *world* or *cosmos* means the universe, awesome in its extension with a multitude of galaxies, each containing billions of stars and planets. The fate of planet earth does not exhaust God's interaction with the world, but our knowledge of the cosmic scope of divine presence is strictly limited. Higher forms of life and spiritual processes are very likely present elsewhere in the cosmos, but the chances of our establishing contact with them are slim. We cannot know about events occurring elsewhere, simultaneously with our own life spans, beyond a few light-years into space. We can see deeply into space only by moving deeply into time. In this sense, we are radically *finite*, subject to the conditions of time and space, which both unify and separate all that is. Yet God, who is *infinite*, must be eternally present and everywhere active.

A new view of the cosmos has been emerging in the natural sciences, especially physics and biology, during the past fifty years. This view opens up the possibility of a unified, nondualistic interpretation of the universe, one that sees the material and spiritual as different aspects of the same reality. Unlike the old, objectifying mechanical *paradigm*, this one reality is described in terms that include aspects of spirituality and subjectivity. We are told that, instead of being made up of tiny material particles, the universe is an open, indeterminate, evolving process that is essentially relational and organic. The dominant paradigm today is that of *relations of energy*, organically interacting and ecologically interdependent, rather than isolated bits of matter. Reality has more the character of event than of substance. The new physics lends itself more readily to a religious interpretation of reality than did the old Newtonian mechanics. So does the new biology if we view chance and randomness not as destructive of all meaning but as instruments by which the potentialities of a universe are run through or explored.

It is ironic that fundamentalist Christians should find the new science so threatening and that they should turn back to an older mechanical model for their creationist account of the origin of the world. Their anachronistic theology with its interventionist God requires an anachronistic science that is actually closer to a seventeenth-century worldview than to that of the Bible. Rather than being viewed as a threat, the new science should be seen as an ally of religion in an exploration of the mysteries of the universe—mysteries that are not subject to empirical description but require for their understanding the use of models and metaphors. The best that we can do is to construct pictures of the world that are shaped not only by experimental evidence but also by language, tacit judgments, hints, and intuitions. In their highest reaches, science and religion, knowledge and faith, merge into a cosmic poetry. Between them are relations of consonance, not of demonstration or proof.

The principal features of the world that emerge from the new scientific paradigm are its *relational-energetic* character, its *organic* interactivity, and its *ecological* interdependence. The presence and activity of God in the world must be understood in terms compatible with these features.

Relations of Energy

Energy (a function of mass and the velocity of light in accord with Einstein's famous formula) is the fundamental material of the cosmos, but it itself is not a stable, measurable substance. According to *quantum theory*, which represents an extension of the general theory of relativity, energy is radiated discontinuously in subatomic units called quanta. These quanta have a dual character, sometimes behaving as waves and sometimes as particles, which are constantly interacting, changing into each other, affecting each other. It is very difficult to think about this unstable, fitful structure, and it is impossible to measure both the position and the momentum of a quantum at one and the same time. This is the principle of indeterminacy or uncertainty, and it points to the fact that reality at the subatomic level is essentially unpicturable.

Energy is the prime metaphor by which this reality is named, but in fact we do not know what it is. The metaphor simply points to something that is active, capable of doing work—in Greek, *energeia*, which comes from the noun for work, *ergon*. Energy has some of the qualities traditionally associated with "spirit"—fluidity, movement, relationality, effective power. When it becomes sufficiently focused, concentrated, inwardly connected, energy takes on the character of mentality. Mind and matter coexist on the same continuum of energy, neither being reducible to the other. They exhibit different modes of relationality, and in ways that we cannot fully grasp they are connected.

The natural world can no longer be viewed as mechanically determined and predictable. Rather, like the mental world, it is a scene of the interplay between chance and necessity, random variation and rulelike regularity, as a consequence of which indeterminacy occurs at the microlevel and unpredictability or noncomputability at the macrolevel. Without chance, there would be no novelty and development; without necessity, there would be no preservation and selection. In brief, the natural world cannot be regarded as static, unchanging, and closed; rather it is dynamic, always in process, a nexus of evolving forms, inexhaustible in its potential for change and novelty. It is not a machine but an organism.

Organic Interactivity

Organic is another metaphor for a feature of the world. It comes from the Greek *organon*, which is also related to *ergon*, and it means something that works through the interaction of parts. Both conceptually and etymologically, it is linked to *energy*, but it stresses the aspect of interactivity in a complex dynamic system. An organism is not necessarily a living thing, but it resembles a living thing in the complexity of its structure and functions. The relations that constitute an organism are internal and mutually affective, with potential for feedback and novelty, by contrast with the external, surface, static relations of a machine.

The cosmos as a whole is an inexhaustibly complex organism. Whether it is also living depends on how broadly or narrowly "life" is defined, and perhaps the distinction between living and nonliving forms is not as important as once was thought. Life is the goal if not the core of the universe. Some cosmologists regard the entire cosmos as a living system. In any event, it is composed of a multitude of dimensions or levels of organization, which are both distinguishable and interactive.

Traditional science tended to erect a reductionistic hierarchy of explanatory relations: the mental (consciousness, thought) is explained in terms of the physiological (the brain), the organic (biology) in terms of the inorganic (chemistry), the atomic in terms of the subatomic (physics). We now know that this view is inadequate. Genuine novelty emerges in each of these dimensions, a novelty that is not reducible to that from which it emerged or evolved. The higher and more complex dimensions of reality are qualitatively distinct; they incorporate the lower dimensions but cannot be explained in the terms appropriate to those lower dimensions.

Reality as a whole is a complex interplay of dimensions, which can neither be reduced to the one-dimensional picture of traditional science nor be divided into the two-dimensional worldview of traditional theology—the supernatural and the natural, the eternal and the temporal, the sacred and the profane. Instead, dimensional analysis should be expanded to include psychological, cultural, ethical, aesthetic, and religious or spiritual aspects of reality, all of which interact in complex ways.

We can never completely grasp what the unity of the cosmic organism consists of because we encounter it only as mediated, never in raw form; because it is not directly observable, we can describe it only metaphorically, not empirically. The favored metaphor at the moment, as we have seen, is that of "energy" or "potency." At the heart of the universe is a potency for creating relations, which arranges itself fluidly and cannot in principle be exhaustively measured, known, and predicted because every attempt to do so interacts with it and thus alters it. If the unitary principle is in some sense energy, then this principle must itself be understood as multidimensional, manifesting itself in a variety of forms ranging from material force to spiritual love. The fundamental theological question is how to understand God in relation to this all-pervasive cosmic *energeia*.

How did the world come to be the complex organism that it is today? The most widely accepted theory is that the universe seems to be expanding from a common origin of about fifteen billion years ago. At the beginning instant, referred to as the "infinite singularity" because it escapes all scientific analysis, the whole universe was the size of an incredibly dense atom. This atom exploded, and within the first fraction of a second the basic gravitational, electromagnetic, and nuclear forces appeared. Although the process of change slowed down considerably after the first three minutes, the universe continued to expand and to develop increasingly rich, diverse, and complex forms, and it is still doing so. At some remotely future time, the cosmos may collapse or disappear into black holes.

Some fascinating parallels exist between this scientific account of origins and the biblical story of creation, which also depicts an absolute beginning and a process of differentiation by which increasing order is drawn from the initial chaos. In both the scientific theory and the biblical myth, the chaos does not simply disappear but remains the fertile ground of novel events, the dynamic source of indeterminacy, flexibility, and freedom. God's Spirit works with this chaos, blows across the face of the waters, sculpting the fluid elements into ordered shapes. Obviously, the story in Genesis does not contain scientific information, nor is it confirmed or disproved by scientific theory. Rather it offers a remarkably intuitive picture of how the world came into being, based on the religious experience of dependence, wonder, order, and contingency.

Ecological Interdependence

The cosmos is not only an organic energy system; it also has an eco-logical aspect. Here yet another metaphor comes into play: *ecology* has something to do with the study (*logos*) of how a house (*oikos*) works. The house in question is our natural home, the earth, as well as *its* home, the cosmic system in which our planet is a tiny speck. Sallie McFague suggests that ecology involves treating the earth as a home rather than a hotel: we take care of a home but use the conveniences of a hotel. Taking care of the earth means recognizing that everything in it is connected in a delicate web of interdependence, and the same is true of the cosmos. Very precise and improbable combinations of elements have permitted the evolution of life on earth and perhaps elsewhere. The exploitation or alteration of one ecosystem, such as forests or atmosphere, has unexpected and often negative conse-quences on other systems, such as rainfall and global temperature. The ecological balances are more finely tuned than once thought, and life has a precious fragility. Traditional religious apprehensions of the world have known this fact intuitively, and today we must struggle to recapture from technological arrogance a respect for the world and a humility in its presence.

An ecological sensibility returns the discussion to the theme of relations, because, as Charles Birch and John Cobb have pointed out, ecology offers a model of internal relations. Thus relations are con-stitutive of entities rather than being something incidental or acci-dental to them. It is not as though entities first exist as self-contained substances and then are subsequently connected with one another. Instead, entities exist only as constituted by relations to other entities in complex and interdependent systems.

Our Western way of thinking is biased toward substances: sub-stances, we assume, are primary realities, and events are the result of the interaction of substances. The ecological model reverses this priority: events are primary, and substantial objects are enduring pat-terns among changing events. Events are the complex interacting of entities, and the latter are simply relations. An entity *is* a mode of relating. This ecological insight bears striking similarities with East-ern, especially Buddhist, ways of thinking, and it offers a point of con-tact for inter-religious dialogue.

The change in sensibility fostered by ecology involves a shift not only from a mechanical-substantial model to an organic-relational model but also from an anthropocentric to a biocentric and cosmocentric perspective. This shift involves a broadening of horizons, not an elimination of concerns for human flourishing. It requires seeing the connection between political justice and ecojustice. It also involves recognizing that the relationship of power and dependence between the human and the natural has been modified by the impact of modern technology. Although we humans were at one time helpless in the face of natural forces, we have now partially mastered them; yet our interference with nature's rhythms may have the ironic effect of increasing nature's destructive forces. The fate of the earth is increasingly in human hands, for good or ill, and we must enlarge our perspective beyond our own needs and desires to a much larger frame of reference. As we contemplate the cosmic horizon and the mystery of our place in it, we find that we are drawn beyond ourselves to the ultimate mystery.

A Creative-Trinitarian View of God

The Divine Creativity

God's being is intrinsically creative being. This is what it means to speak of God, in Paul Tillich's terms, as "being-itself" or the "power of being." Being is not an entity or substance but a *power* or a *potency*, a letting-be by which everything that is exists. As the power of being, God is radically transcendent, qualitatively distinct from every finite entity and the totality of finite entities, the world. At the same time, God is radically immanent, for every finite entity participates in or depends on being-itself. Otherwise it would have no *power* of being and would be swallowed up in nonbeing. Being-itself is not a common substance in all beings or an independent substance apart from beings. It is pure power—pure creative and relational power—which is qualitatively distinct from all things as the power upon which they are radically dependent for their being, yet which is available only in and through finite things.

The theological tradition established two symbols of God's worldly power—creation and *providence*—but these can be seen as two aspects of the same reality, as Langdon Gilkey and others have pointed out. Creation symbolizes God as the sole ground of all that is; providence symbolizes God's ongoing preservation and ordering as it unfolds through temporal process. Providence is a continuous divine creativity; if it is appropriate to think of creation as an ongoing dynamic process rather than something that happened once-and-for-all at the beginning, then creation has a providential, caring quality, and providence is the ever-new creativity of God. Linking creation and providence is an implication of understanding God in dynamic and relational terms. A more difficult task is that of understanding *how* God acts creatively and providentially in the world.

The proposal I offer in this book is that God's creative power of being manifests itself in different modalities in different dimensions of the created world. In the physical-chemical-biological dimension, the power of being appears as a primal and all-pervasive *energy*. In the dimension of consciousness, history, and spirit, it appears as the creative and saving power of *language*. These dimensions interpenetrate rather than being externally related. Language is a refinement or inwardizing concentration of the radial power of energy. In the modalities of both energy and language, God's creative power is shaping, forming, *ideal* power, the primordial power of *pure possibility*. It is present in, yet distinct from, natural and human powers: it empowers these powers.

Let us try to imagine God's creative power of being as a *primal energy* or potency working at all levels of the evolutionary scale, including the human, granting being to the world and drawing it toward certain ends and values. In the organic dimension, broadly understood, we can imagine God's power as affording an infinite number of possibilities for novelty and for the enhancement of value and life. Some of these possibilities become actual in nature through accidental mutations in the chemical structure of genes. When a combination of such mutations creates a more viable organism, that organism prevails through natural selection. According to molecular biology, this is the secret of evolution, an interplay of chance and necessity, random variation and lawlike uniformity.

We need not understand this process as utterly devoid of purpose, for the most potentially fruitful source of innovation is random variation. Computers simulate creativity by generating a large number of possibilities of response, enabling the most appropriate ones to be selected. If we wish to affirm that God acts creatively in the universe, then chance and random variation, far from being antithetical to divine purpose, are essential instruments of it. Chance itself is not creative but provides the space or vehicle of creativity. Creativity is the work of God, of God's power of being. Any reference to "creativity" entails a perspective that transcends natural science.

According to the philosopher of "process," Alfred North Whitehead, the infinite possibilities for novelty in the world, which are possibilities for a fuller and richer actualization of being, are contained in (indeed constitute) the primordial nature of God. Hence Whitehead called these possibilities "ideals" and proposed that a "relevant" ideal is offered to each occasion of experience (a unit of energy in the natural world, ranging from subatomic particles to moments of human consciousness), by which its potentialities can be maximized, although this ideal is only occasionally seized on and enacted. Apart from ideals, the world tends toward repetition, drift, and disorder, or what physicists call *entropy*. The causality exercised by God is not that of a *first cause* or a material cause, which bring about specific, predetermined effects, but that of a *final cause*, which offers a possibility, an invitation, a goal. God's creative power also works as a *formal cause*, providing patterns or ideals for the shaping of events, but not controlling outcomes. Final and formal causes exercise real influence within a framework of contingency, freedom, and indeterminacy. God orders the world, orients it to the attainment of value, but God does not mechanically control the dynamics of the creative process.

When energy becomes sufficiently concentrated and inwardized, it takes on the character of consciousness, thought, speech, intentional action, all of which are linguistic in character. This is the distinctive form that cosmic energy assumes for human beings, and God's creative power must manifest itself in linguistic forms if it is to be efficacious for humans. Thus God appears as a saving Word spoken in and through the drift of human words and as a transformative Wisdom that appears in and through the foolishness of human thought and practice. The divine Word and Wisdom appear as the power of truth, insight, liberation, and new possibility amid the deception, folly, oppression, and repetitiveness that characterize human speech and action in the everyday world.

Language and thought are the most powerful instruments in the cosmos, but they are limited by their inexorable finitude and have been corrupted by human sin. When a truthful and liberating word is spoken or a revelatory insight occurs in the babel of voices and ideologies that make up human history, we experience such a word and wisdom as a *saving, transformative gift*, a gift beyond our capacity to produce and our worthiness to have. We remain at its disposal rather than disposing it. Christians attribute this gift to the *Word* and *Wisdom of God*, to a divine liberating power that transcends every human capacity but that works through ordinary human voices and deeds.

God's creative power of being is not simply identical with cosmic energy and human linguisticality. God works *within* energy to render it creative and upbuilding, resisting its destructive and wayward tendencies. God works *within* language to lure it toward freedom, truth, and love, resisting its oppressive, deceitful, and alienating tendencies. Thus I have spoken of the divine power of being as a *primal* energy, a *saving* Word, a *transformative* Wisdom. These are metaphorical ways of designating God's being-in-the-world. The adjective *primal* means that God's being exercises an ideal, life-enhancing, goal-directed primordial power within cosmic energy; the adjectives *saving* and *transformative* mean that God's Word and Wisdom evoke, measure, and redeem human speaking and thinking.

By creating it, God sets the world free to move by its own inner dynamisms, which have both creative and tragic potentials. God does not control these dynamisms but works through them toward life-enhancing and justice-producing ends. God's power of being has the quality of *ideality*, of pure possibility, by contrast with the materiality of cosmic energy and human speech. It is an ideal that works *within* the material, a spiritual power that indwells the natural world. It works rather as a *purpose* does with material resources. Purposive action makes use of natural processes, leaving them to function in their own way but achieving a goal they cannot possibly envision. The philosopher of *idealism* G. W. F. Hegel understood this to be the way that God providentially governs the world. God's purpose is to achieve harmony, goodness, and wisdom from the waywardness, evil, and folly of the world.

God as the One Who
Has the Power of Being Absolutely

What is the relationship of God to the power of being that works in the world as primal energy and saving, transformative language? Is God simply identical with this power or in some way different from it? If God is simply identical with the power of being, God seems to be made into a process, a relationality, a creativity—but then God is not a creator, a personal agent, a subject, and a vital aspect of religious faith and experience has been lost. It is difficult to imagine praying to a serendipitous creativity. Thinking of God as a person, it might be argued, is a comforting and perhaps necessary illusion. Religions have lived by this illusion, for the widely accepted view is that God is a Supreme Being who exists, as it were, on the other side of or beyond worldly being. To think of God as *a* being, however, is to reduce God to the status of a worldly entity, even if God is regarded as the *Supreme* Being, the metaphysical first cause. To think of God as a Supreme Being is still to think of God in finite terms: God is the biggest, the oldest, the most powerful, the wisest being imaginable. Such a being is what Hegel called a "spurious infinite," which is merely an indefinitely extended finite. Theism is the doctrine that God is a Supreme Being; but the true God, Tillich argues, is the God beyond the God of theism.

We seem, then, to have arrived at an impasse in thinking about the relationship between God and being: God is neither the power of being nor a Supreme Being. Many theologians insist that the problem arises from the very project of thinking the relationship between God and being, which (they say) is a relationship that cannot be thought. God is an ultimate mystery whose mode of being remains beyond human comprehension. All categories applied to God break down—whether those of being, person, event, power, energy, love, becoming, nonbeing, or emptiness. There is a profound truth to this insight, which reminds us that before all talk about God there is silence, mystery, and holiness. A negative or apophatic moment must be present in every theology. But God does come forth into speech, and religions are filled with God-talk, which needs to be analyzed and disciplined in some fashion, not simply silenced.

In thinking about the relationship between God and being, I have been helped by an ingenious proposal by the twentieth-century

Catholic theologian Karl Rahner (who in turn was influenced by the philosophy of Martin Heidegger): God is "the being that has being absolutely." The being that has being *absolutely* is no longer simply a (supreme) being but *is* being, that is, the event or power of being. Thus Rahner can speak of God as "pure being" or "absolute being," just as Tillich speaks of God as "being-itself." Rahner, however, insists that such speech be understood as shorthand for the clumsy expression "the being that has being absolutely": being is always the being of some actual being or society of beings; the power of being is the pure *possibility* of being and cannot be thought of apart from that which it enables to be, even as it must not be confused with what it enables to be, namely beings or finite entities. It is a *potency*, not an entity. For this reason, it is nonbeing as much as being, emptiness as much as fullness.

Rahner's formula makes it clear that the power of being is at the *disposal* of God, who has it absolutely, whereas all finite beings are at *being's* disposal. To have the power of being *absolutely* means to be able to release it, to let it go into the world, to *absolve* it. This idea is suggested by a play on the root sense of the word *absolute* (from the Latin verb *absolvere*), which means to "absolve," "loosen," "release," "let go." As absolute, God is not something independent or isolated, cut off from everything finite, as we tend to think; rather God is relational, releasing the divine power, giving rise to what is other than God, namely, the world. God has and gives being absolvingly. Moreover, God is related internally rather than externally to that to which God gives being. The world is not a "beyond" to God, something that stands outside the divine relationality and by which God is limited. Instead, the world has the quality of otherness *within* the divine life. This is another aspect of the absoluteness of God, and as such is a mark of the divine freedom: God gives being freely and remains free in relation to what has been given being. God's infinity includes the finitude of the world within itself.

I find it helpful to reformulate Rahner's statement as follows: God is "*the One who* has *the power of* being absolutely." A simpler version of the latter still-clumsy phrase is "the One who lets be," for the power of being is just what lets beings be. The simpler version approximates the divine name given in Exod. 3:14. The mystery of the name is safeguarded in the *tetragrammaton* YHWH, which is connected with the

Hebrew verb *hayah*, "to be." YHWH means "I am who I am" or "I am the One who lets be." As such, YHWH is "the One who has being absolutely."

The proposed modification makes clearer the distinction between the two senses of *being*—an actual personal *subject* on the one hand (the One), and a process, event, or power of letting-be on the other. In the case of God and God alone, these two senses absolutely cohere. In a way that we cannot fully grasp, God is *both*—both a noun and a verb, both actuality and potentiality, both personal subject and creative-redemptive power. God is not *any* personal subject but *the* personal subject who has, disposes, releases the power of being absolutely and who therefore, in a way we cannot adequately express, *is* this very power. Thus God is both personal and suprapersonal. God is the one true and perfect *person*—not *a* person but *the* person, *personhood*, or (to use a term coined by Samuel Taylor Coleridge) *personeity*. Because God has this power absolutely, God is distinguished qualitatively from all finite persons. God is not a finite subject but infinite subjectivity—which is really *intersubjectivity*, a communicative interplay of subjects. God's absolute being is social, not isolated and singular, being. Elaboration of this idea requires turning to the doctrine of the Trinity.

The Triune Life of God

A Trinity is implicit in the formulation, "the One who has the power of being absolutely." "The One" is, in the traditional *conceptuality* of trinitarian theology, the Creator, the "Father almighty, maker of heaven and earth," the beginning and end of all things. "The power of being," which is the power of divine creativity, is the essential attribute of the Son, the Logos, the Wisdom of God, eternally active in the creation and redemption of the world. And the adverb "absolutely" points to the Holy Spirit as the qualifier of the relationship between God and the world, designating the absolving divine relationality and freedom—the freedom to let the world go in its finitude and independence and the freedom to remain God in relation to the world. The Spirit constitutes the matrix of interactivity between God and the world.

First, God is God in and for godself. Then distinction is introduced into the divine life, for God lets be what is not God—the world.

Yet what is not God, the world, remains an element within the divine life, for God is not an entity but a process that encompasses both identity and difference, oneness and manyness, ideality and reality. Thus the distinction between God and the world generates *three* rather than two relational figures or gestalts: God's self-identity apart from the world, the creative act by which difference is established between God and the world, and the interaction of God and the world by which an inclusive whole is generated. This insight lies at the core of the doctrine of the Trinity.

In elaborating this insight, I propose to avoid the traditional designation of divine "persons" of the Trinity who are named "Father," "Son," and "Holy Spirit." Two central problems crop up with this language. First, it is *patriarchal* and *hierarchical*. It encourages us to think of God as three male beings arranged in a definite rank, from the Father (the supreme authority) to the Son and thence to the Spirit, whose standing in the Trinity was never clearly explained by the tradition and who remained subordinated to the other persons. Second, the language is *mythological*. It encourages us to think of God as three persons or personal agencies who interact with one another in a divine society and who make supernatural appearances in history. The Latin term *persona*, and its Greek equivalents, *prosopon* and *hypostasis*, which were employed in the ancient debates about the Trinity, did not mean "person" in the modern sense of a self-conscious ego but referred rather to the role or persona assumed by an actor. Something of this ancient sense might be captured by speaking, like the nineteenth-century Reformed theologian Horace Bushnell, of the divine personae as "personifications" or "impersonations" of God in the world. God becomes configured in distinctive shapes, figures, or gestalts associated with distinctive modes of being of the one personal God in relation to godself and to the world.

In searching for a nonmythological and nonpatriarchal way of naming these gestalts, I propose to think, first, of *God within godself simply as God*, the One; second, as *God in the world in Christ*, that is, in processes of creative transformation mediated through Christ and other redemptive figures; and third, as *God and the world together in the Spirit*. The names *God*, *Christ*, and *Spirit* are, to be sure, metaphorical and quasi-personal, but they need not assume mythological and patriarchal overtones. They designate relationships rather than personal entities, but they employ the concrete language of scripture and liturgy rather than the abstract language of philosophy. I prefer to call them *figures* or *gestalts* rather than "persons." The divine personae are gestalts constituted by relationships; the divine life as a whole is a triune configuration of these gestalts. *Gestalt* is a loan word from German, designating an integrated structure or pattern, and it seems well-suited to name the integrated patterns that make up the triune God.

To think of God within godself points to another classical trinitarian distinction, that between the *immanent* and *economic* Trinities. The *immanent Trinity* was thought to be composed of the interplay of the Father, Son, and Holy Spirit within the divine life before and apart from God's creation of the world; it was principally the immanent Trinity that was intended by the doctrine of the Trinity. The *economic Trinity* was derivative. It was a way of designating God's creative and redemptive work in the world, in the divine *oikonomia* or work of salvation. The adjective *economic* in this context has an odd ring to modern ears, and it is conceptually misleading if it implies two separate Trinities. A better expression is that of "inclusive Trinity." That is, the triune life of God *includes* both the immanent Trinity (God's internal self-relatedness) and God's creative-transformative-consummating work in the world as designated by the symbols of Christ and Spirit.

The model I propose accords primacy to the inclusive rather than to the immanent Trinity; it employs metaphors of relationships rather than of persons; it is interactive rather than hierarchical, *pneumatocentric* rather than *logocentric*, spiraling rather than linear. All of this requires spelling out in some detail, with help from Augustine, Aquinas, Hegel, and Barth.

Figures of the Trinity:
The Interaction of God and the World

"God": God within Godself as the One

God is in the first instance the One who is primordially self-identical. This is the most elemental meaning of the word *God* for Judaism and Christianity. It was the great accomplishment of Israelite faith to attain for the first time the meaning of the word God as "the One."

God is not strictly a name but the circumlocution for a name, in the case of Israel the tetragrammaton YHWH, "the One who lets be." The one God is not, however, an undifferentiated monad or substance. God is already, in the first moment of the divine life, a subject-event or person-event, an act or process or spiral of self-distinguishing and self-relating that cannot be derived from or traced to anything other than itself. In this respect God is "unbegotten," *a se*, from godself.

If God is not in this respect self-generating, then it is difficult to avoid the conclusion that God is generated from something other than God, namely, the world or cosmic process. The function of the moment of identity in the doctrine of the Trinity is to establish the ontological priority of God vis-à-vis the world. *God* is the creator, not the world; God is the One who has the power of being absolutely. Thus the immanent Trinity should not be displaced by the economic or inclusive Trinity, as many modern theologians have argued, but encompassed within it as a necessary generative moment.

Obviously we have no direct knowledge of the inner life of God, which remains an inexhaustible mystery for us. We encounter God as God comes forth in the world in a threefold spiraling pattern—creator, creativity, consummation—and from this we reflect on the being of God. We are able to think of the immanent Trinity analogically and imaginatively on the basis of our own limited experience of personal identity and self-relatedness, but we produce models and metaphors, not literal descriptions. If God does not depend on the world to be God, then we must assume that there subsists within God a core of self-relatedness.

To be a self requires being related to an other-than-self in which one finds one's own self reflected back to oneself. Selfhood entails a self and an other and a relationship between them. The other is normally another self, but human beings also find themselves reflected back to themselves through encounters with nature. No human being can subsist without such outwardly experienced relationships. Just this, we may conjecture, is what is different about God: God is in the first instance God's *own other*. As Karl Barth says, in the event by which God is God, God is subject, object, and predicate, or revealer, revealed, and act of revelation. In Hegelian terms, God is identity, difference, and mediation. This means that God does not depend on an other-than-God to be a subject, a person. God is sufficient unto godself, and this constitutes God's holiness, sublimity, and mystery.

Precisely this self-sufficiency is the condition of possibility of God's entering into relationship with an other that is not God in such a way that the autonomy and independence of the other are allowed to stand and are not utterly absorbed into God's own being. It is for the sake of the world, for the sake of the world's finite freedom, that God's creation of the world is free and unexacted, a purely gratuitous gift, and it can be so only insofar as in the first instance God is God's own other. We know from our own experience that if we are not in some sense self-constituting, if we are utterly dependent on others to be the persons that we are, then we either lose ourselves or destroy others in what are called co-dependency relationships. What is partially true of us is wholly true of God, who is both utterly absolute and utterly related in a way we can only faintly grasp. The distinction between absoluteness and relativity disappears in the divine personeity, for God is absolute precisely in being utterly self-related and utterly world related; to be both is to be utterly personal. Of course, *our* self-constituting is always preceded by something else, namely, the nexus of world relations; we cannot exist independently of the world. God's self-constituting act, however, is not preceded by anything other than itself.

The word *God* designates the oneness, the unity, the wholeness, the sublimity, the *aseity* of God, the One on whom all things depend and in whom they find their final fulfillment. It is not surprising that the parental terms "Father" and "Mother" appear in scriptural and liturgical language to name God as God. The figure of the mother was a dominant image of divinity in many ancient religions throughout the world. The father may be the begetter, but it is the mother who gives birth and nurtures, and there is no more powerful image of divine origination than that of the great matrix or womb from which everything comes forth. Something of this imagery is expressed in the Hebrew Bible where God is figured as mother, midwife, nurse, lover, teacher, wisdom (*sophia*). Israel, however, developed into a patriarchal society dominated by kings, prophets, rabbis, and fathers, and the maternal imagery was suppressed in favor of thinking and speaking of God in masculine terms—a practice that has continued in the Christian West to the present day and that has been seriously questioned only in recent years.

Despite its evocative power, parental imagery used of God has seriously distorting effects. It does not help to think of God as a gendered being, male or female, and the relationship between God and the world is not really analogous to that between a parent and a child. For the first figure of the divine life, I prefer the simple yet inexhaustible word "God."

"Christ": God in the World as Creative-Redemptive Love

By an act of gratuitous love, God posits externally the moment of distinction and difference that is already implicit within God. God goes out from godself, creates a world seemingly infinite in its extension but strictly nondivine in its perishability and contingency, yet enters into relationship with that world, makes it God's own "body," becomes embodied or incarnate in it, suffers its *estrangement*, conflict, death, but also works toward its reconciliation, renewal, salvation. Thereby the nonserious "play of love with itself," by which Hegel characterized the immanent Trinity, becomes deadly serious. The absolute is "released" into "the seriousness of other-being, of separation and rupture." In the world, it is interrupted, broken, "dismembered." God becomes a tragic God but also sublates tragedy, overcomes tragic conflict.

God's love is a *free* love because it is not necessitated by the creature and is purely gratuitous. The freedom of God indicates that the relationship between God and the world is first strictly a divine action, the ever-original divine act of self-distinction, self-othering, self-giving. But it is also the case that God *needs* the world in order to become fully the God that God is capable of becoming—not locked into a self-enclosed unity as the abstract isolated One but opening up the divine self to encompass genuine otherness, becoming thereby concrete and spiritual, being no longer simply the One but the All in all. Ernst Troeltsch referred to this idea as God's capacity to grow and characterized it as "the self-augmentation of God." This growth is intrinsic to the very being of God, not an outwardly imposed necessity; the necessity is internal and thus identical with God's freedom to be God. Our formulation at this point can only be dialectical: God is in the first instance God's own other, yet God needs the otherness of the world created by God to extend and complete God's own otherness. (In a similarly dialectical fashion, God is humanity's wholly other, yet is also the friend who appears in the face of Jesus.)

If the world is created merely for God to have an object to love, an other that augments the divine life, is it not reduced to being a function of God and lacking intrinsic value of its own? To counteract this danger, we must believe that God creates for the sake of the creature as well as the creator and that God really does grant the world its own inviolable otherness and independence. The world is an end in itself as well as having an end in God. Tragically, insofar as it cuts itself off from God, the world converts its divinely given otherness into a structure of domination and oppression, of "us" versus "them," of forced otherness. Yet God does not abandon the world to its otherness; indeed God is present in a special way to those who become "the others" of history—the sick and impoverished, the scorned and rejected. God's love not only frees the world to be other but liberates it from the alienating otherness it imposes on itself.

Christ, a title taken from Jewish messianic expectation, is the symbol or figure by which Christians understand God's creative and redemptive presence in the world. Classical Christology connected Christ with the eternal *Logos* or *Wisdom of God* by which God creates and governs the world. The symbol *Christ* also profoundly connects God with the finitude, contingency, perishability, and death of the world. Christians believe that the death of Christ on the cross is the very death of God, and also that with the *resurrection* of Christ, as Paul wrote, the perishable puts on imperishability, and death is swallowed up in victory (1 Cor. 15:54).

To say that God suffers death and takes the perishability of the world into the divine life can mean only that the world as such becomes an element within the divine life. The world is by no means divinized in this process; on the contrary, just the opposite is the case because it is precisely the perishability of the world, its nondivine character, that is taken into the divine life. When the perishable "puts on" the imperishable, it does not cease to be perishable. Rather (following an insight of Eberhard Jüngel) its annihilating nothingness is converted into the possibility of the new. It becomes "the differentiating power in the identity of being." By taking on the perishable, God's own being is historicized, becomes a being-in-process. The

world remains precisely the moment of difference, negation, otherness, finitude, perishability—the realm of ongoing struggle between
creativity and destructiveness, good and evil—within the triune configuration of God.

Thus the cosmic significance of the figure of Christ is that the
world as a whole is destined to become God's body. Such a claim
should not be regarded as a crude *pantheism* that confuses all things
with God and divinizes physical and human nature. The world is precisely *not*-God, and *because* it is not-God it is a moment within the
divine life. The extraordinary thing about God is that God over-
reaches and incorporates what is not-God within God. God is the
identity of God and not-God, the event that takes place between God
and the world. Thereby God is a God whose being is in process, and
what is not-God has the possibility of being saved from its annihilating nothingness. The world fulfills its role within the divine life only
by remaining other than God. If it were reduced to the same, all real
difference would evaporate, and God would be, in Robert Williams's
words, a "bloodless abstraction—solitary, lifeless, and alone like
Aristotle's unmoved mover, or the Neo-Platonic One." If a label is
required for such a view, it is *panentheism* or *holism*, not pantheism.

Christ is not only a cosmic but also a historical figure. Christians
believe that "Christ," meaning God's power of creative and redemptive love, became incarnate in Jesus of Nazareth and that the
distinctive features of Jesus' life, ministry, death, and resurrection paradigmatically configure God's redemptive love in the world. Just how
we are to interpret the incarnation of Christ in Jesus of Nazareth is the
task of chapter 5. For now I want to emphasize that Jesus is one among
a plurality of revelatory religious figures. Human beings live in a diversity of cultures and religions, and we must believe that God becomes
concretely and redemptively present in each of the great cultural trajectories in ways appropriate to each. In addition to Jesus, we recognize Abraham and Moses, Muhammad, Buddha, Krishna, and Gandhi,
to name but a few. In our own culture, we recognize that Christ is not
one but many: both history and literature bear testimony to the presence of Christ figures, *saints* both sacred and secular, who bear witness
to Jesus of Nazareth yet differ from him. One of the features of the
world is simply its rich and irreducible diversity. If Christians wish to
claim that it is the Christic principle that appears not only in Jesus but

in other religious figures as well, it must be acknowledged that this is a Christian perspective on the whole and that other religions have other names for a mystery that transcends all naming.

Not only is Jesus one among several paradigmatic religious figures of world-historical significance, but through the very particularities of his life and death—his proclamation of the kingdom of God, his crucifixion, his living presence to the community of faith—he points beyond himself to the world as a whole. The particular figure of Jesus of Nazareth disappears into his ministry, takes the misery of the world literally into himself, suffers in its place in such a way that his own identity merges with that of the world. He points beyond himself not only to God and God's kingdom but also to the community of brothers and sisters, the little community of table fellowship and the great community of disciples through all ages. His personal, ethnic, sexual, cultural, historical, and religious specificities are taken up into a new corporate, intersubjective embodiment that cuts across all provincial modes of existence and whose goal is simply the world as such.

Thus Christ and the world are figures of God's creative-redemptive love at opposite ends of a continuum, each presupposing and completing the other. Christ is (for Christians) the revelatory clue to the world as an ambiguous process; the world is the goal of the emancipatory praxis that arises from Christ's life and death. "Christ" is shorthand for "God-in-the-world-in-Christ" and "God-in-Christ-in-the-world." God is in Christ as the representative human being, the "son of humanity" (*huios tou anthrōpou*). Precisely his not-God-ness, his common identity with the world, is the bearer of divinity. What makes him Christ is not a privileged, superhuman divine nature but utter identification with the anguish and joy of human nature. It is the intensity of his humanity that radiates divinity; it is as "son of humanity" that he is "son of God."

Christ ("the anointed or messianic one") is a symbol that is particular to the Jewish and Christian traditions. *Spirit* is a more universally available religious symbol, and it has the culminating place in the triad of symbols by which Christians identify God. It helps to open Christian trinitarian theology to a genuine religious pluralism. *Spirit* is the most encompassing of the divine figures, incorporating God as *God* and God as *Christ*. It emerges from the interaction of God and the world; it expresses, indeed *is*, that very interaction.

"Spirit": God and the World
Together in Consummate Freedom

The act of creation by which God distinguishes a world from godself is not the final act. There is also an act of consummation by which God brings an alienated and fallen world back into communion with godself. If love is the power of difference, freedom is the power of mediation and communion; but love and freedom, differentiation and reunification, are inseparable. Difference occurs for the sake of a richer unity, and mediation preserves and cherishes differences. God is free love and loving freedom—or, as Karl Barth says, the One who loves in freedom. *Freedom* is not simply the capacity to choose options voluntarily. It is much richer than that: it is a consummated presence-to-self mediated in and through presence-to-others. Thus it presupposes love's positing of distinction and completes love's act of reunion. The divine freedom is not sheer indeterminacy but is determined by and bound to compassion for the world. Because this compassion is an aspect of the divine freedom, it is not left hanging in the anguish of death and separation but is completed by God's overcoming estrangement, negating the annihilating power of death, re-establishing communion by the "subjection" and return of all things, "that God may be all in all" (1 Cor. 15:28).

Freedom thus means both the perfection of God and the liberation of the world. These are often thought of as topics for *eschatology*, the doctrine of "last things," but they refer to processes that, while pointing toward the future, are presently at work in the world. Freedom is the perfection of God because God simply *is* freedom—free love and loving freedom. Freedom means the mediation and thus the completion of all relationships. Perfect freedom means the consummation of all relationships in God, whose being is one of inclusive and absolute relationality. This is God as Spirit.

The liberation of the world is the purpose or goal of God's love for the world. God loves the world toward an end, which is that of shaping scenes of freedom from the repeated scenes of domination that make up world history. In history, these configurations of freedom are fragmentary, ambiguous, incomplete, and the configuring process is as endless as the disfiguring one. In this endless process, however, the world has an end, a *telos*, in the sense not of a chronologically future consummation but of a goal or purpose, which infuses and transforms the process. This end is the liberation of the world in God, which occurs by means of subduing or subjecting the world's endless, restless, creative-destructive difference in the eternal peace and unity of God. This process is going on all the time; it is not reserved for some future end. It gives the world future and new possibility and enables fragmentary shapes of freedom to survive and sometimes to prevail against scenes of violence and domination. The ground of redemptive praxis in the world is the liberation of the world in God, and this in turn is the perfection of God's freedom. The return of all things to God is a transhistorical consummation that infuses and energizes the historical process in every moment of present time.

What name designates the final figure of the *triune configuration*? The tradition named it *Spirit*, which, unlike *Father* and *Son*, is a retrievable symbol for the postmodern context. Spirit is not something abstract and dualistic, as is commonly thought, but is concrete and unifying. In most languages, the word *spirit* has etymological associations with natural forces—breath, wind, air, light, fire, water—forces that themselves are vital and that give life, "the breath of life." Spirit is what is alive, active, energetic, moving, fluid, but spirit is also what is rational and conscious. In the Hebraic and Christian traditions, Spirit is closely associated with the figures of Wisdom (*Sophia*) and Word (*Logos*), which are its bearers or manifestations for human life. Spirit is in fact the unity of nature and reason, body and soul, vitality and mentality. It assumes the form of both primal energy and saving, transformative language. We can now name the power of being by which God creates and redeems the world as "Spirit."

God is Spirit insofar as God is present to, active in, embodied by that which is other than God, namely, the natural and human worlds. Thus in scripture, Spirit refers to that modality of divine activity whereby God indwells and empowers the forces of nature, the people of Israel, the ecclesial community, and individual persons (above all, Jesus of Nazareth). Spirit is the indwelling power of God, which brings the natural and human worlds to consummation by bringing estranged and fallen beings into everlasting, liberating communion with the one God, whose true and proper name is now

Spirit. Thus Spirit is already present and at work in the second moment, the moment of creation and differentiation, but it is fully recognized only in the third moment, the moment of liberation and consummation. This is because Spirit is an *emergent* figure; it emerges from the interaction of God and the world. I return to these themes in chapter 6.

The relationship between Christ and the Spirit is complex. The Spirit both precedes Christ and follows Christ. Spirit, in the shape of Logos or Wisdom, is the power that indwells or "inspirits" Jesus of Nazareth, making him the Christ, the anointed one of Israel, who does not triumph but is crucified, thereby becoming a different savior figure. The specific configuration of compassionate, liberating, redemptive power in Jesus Christ defines the Spirit and provides a basis for distinguishing between divine and demonic forms of spiritual power. In this sense, Christ sends the Spirit into the church and the world for the purpose of taking up and completing his mission. Yet the Spirit transcends Christ and appears in a diversity of religious figures and traditions, which also contribute to the delineation and enrichment of spirituality. Thus we cannot say exhaustively what Spirit is: Spirit is both concretely configured and open to new possibilities.

The theological tradition never found a proper place for the Spirit. The logic of the tradition tended to be binary rather than triadic and viewed the Holy Spirit as an appendage to the Father and the Son, a subordinate instrument in the economy of salvation. By contrast, I agree with Tillich that Spirit is the richest, most encompassing, and least restricted of the trinitarian symbols. In his last lectures on the philosophy of religion, Hegel said: "The abstractness of the Father is given up in the Son—this then is death. But the negation of this negation is the unity of Father and Son—love, or the Spirit." In other words, the abstract God, the Supreme Being, the Father, dies in the death of the Son, a particular male human being; both Father and Son are reborn as concrete, world-encompassing Spirit. The abstract oneness of God and the specific incarnation of God are not lost but preserved in a richer, more inclusive unity. This logic is not binary and linear but triadic and spiraling, moving interactively through God and the world into Spirit. The two models can be represented diagrammatically as follows:

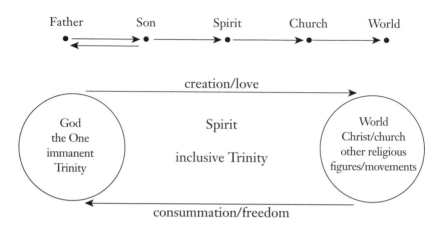

In the first model, the movement of salvation is linear, *from* the Father *through* the Son *in* the Spirit *to* the church and thence *into* the world. The model is *christocentric* and *ecclesiocentric* in the sense that the saving work is done by the Son, who is of the same substance with the Father, and the place of salvation is properly the church. The Holy Spirit proceeds from the Father and the Son, but they are not comparably dependent on it. Rather the Spirit is a link between Christ and the church, whereas the church has a mission to Christianize the world, to bring it into line.

In the second model, the circles should be viewed not as closed circuits but as open spirals, and Spirit forms a spiraling mediation between God and world: thus the model is *pneumatocentric* and dynamic. (It is difficult to represent the spiraling diagrammatically without a third dimension that leaps off the page.) Redemption transpires in the world through diverse religiocultural vehicles in which spiritual power is recognized to be at work, but Christ and the church retain their relative validity and contribute to a greater whole.

The first model is masculine and patriarchal; the second attempts to avoid gender specificity. The noun *God* is masculine grammatically but not conceptually, and the challenge is to liberate our thinking and speaking about God from gendered associations without losing a sense of the divine personhood. *Christ* is masculine insofar as it is a title for the Jewish Messiah and for Jesus of Nazareth, but it has the potential for transcending gender specificity through its association with a diversity of figures and communities.

Spirit is neither masculine nor feminine. Among the traditional trinitarian symbols, it has the advantage of providing a way of naming God that is not patriarchal and gender specific. The word for *Spirit* is feminine in Hebrew, masculine in Latin, and neuter in Greek. Thus it is gender transcendent, but pronominal references to it are inescapably gendered. I have used the neuter singular pronoun, but perhaps plural forms would be more appropriate because Spirit is essentially a communal, intersubjective figure, a personal gestalt emerging from many persons and indeed from the whole of nature. Spirit is plural, fluid, emergent, and interactive. Spirit is "we"—the wholeness toward which the oneness of God is pointing.

EXERCISES

1. For nearly two millennia, Christians have thought of God as sovereign Lord of the universe. At the beginning of the third millennium, is it really necessary to question the "logic of divine sovereignty" and attempt to find an "interactive" alternative?

2. A typical class or group is likely to have several people who are well-informed about natural science. Let these people talk briefly about recent developments in the science with which they are familiar, and let other members of the class press for clarifications and implications for religious faith. Alternatively, read and discuss one of the recent books on religion and science listed in the bibliography for chapters 1 and 3.

3. The first section of this chapter (pp. 48–54) argues for a coherence between the new scientific cosmologies that emerged in the twentieth century and the biblical way of understanding the origin of the world and God's activity in the world. Furthermore, the claim is made that creationism presupposes an older, anachronistic science that describes the world as a machine rather than an organism. Form two groups, one of which defends the coherence between postmodern science and religion advocated in this book and the other of which challenges it. What critical theological issues are at stake in this debate?

4. Try thinking of reality in relational rather than substantial terms. In other words, relations or events are primary, not entities or

substances. Substantial objects (such as the human self or the divine being) are enduring patterns among changing events. How difficult or easy is it for you to think in these terms? What cherished assumptions have to be given up, and what new insights are obtained? Write a brief thought experiment in which you allow your imagination to explore the implications of a relational view, or engage in a spiritual exercise along these lines. Exchange what you have written with similar efforts by other members of your class.

5. The second section of the chapter (pp. 54–62) sets forth a proposal about the *being* of God, with *being* understood as the power of letting-be, that is, as purely creative power, the primordial power of pure possibility, which works in and through worldly powers, moving or luring the world toward certain ends, purposes, values. Many people might argue that it is wrong in principle to connect "God" (a personal religious symbol) with "being" (an abstract philosophical concept). Such a connection, they say, smacks of natural theology (based on philosophical or scientific observations of the world) as opposed to revealed theology (what is disclosed about God in scripture). Form several small groups in which you debate the pros and cons of this issue. Share your conclusions with the larger class.

6. What problems attach to thinking of God as either "a Supreme Being" (a person) or "being-itself" (a power)? Do you agree with the argument of the chapter for a third alternative, namely thinking of God as "the One who has the power of being absolutely"? Does this alternative avoid the difficulties or simply multiply them?

7. Imagine yourself in a discussion with a group of people who are well-informed about the modern world but have become doubtful about their religious conviction. How would you introduce the "God-question"? What questions would you ask? What points would you want to emphasize? Do you think any consensus might emerge as to the reality of God?

8. "Thus the distinction between God and the world generates *three* rather than two relational figures or gestalts: God's self-identity apart from the world, the creative act by which difference is established between God and the world, and the interaction of God and the world by which an inclusive whole is generated. This insight

lies at the core of the doctrine of the Trinity" (see p. 61). How well does this proposal fit with the traditional doctrine of three divine Persons: Father, Son, and Holy Spirit? Why not continue to use the traditional trinitarian names and to think of the Trinity as one substance in three persons? Why not abandon trinitarian thinking entirely and emphasize the oneness of God? These questions could be debated by forming three groups, one of which defends classical trinitarianism, another the unitarian option, and a third the reconstruction proposed in this chapter. (On classical trinitarianism, see J. N. D. Kelly, *Early Christian Doctrines*, chaps. 4–5, 10).

9. Today the tendency is to say that nothing can be known of God's innermost being and self-relatedness. What we know is how God appears and acts in the world, and this knowledge tends to be practical rather than theoretical. Thus the immanent Trinity is regarded as unwarranted theological speculation, and attention is focused on the so-called economic Trinity, God's creation, governance, and redemption of the world. This book is opposed to this tendency. Evaluate the success or failure of its argument. On what grounds can we truly *know* anything at all about God?

10. What sense do you make of the statement that "the world is precisely *not*-God, and *because* it is not-God it is a moment within the divine life"? Or of the statement that "God over-reaches and incorporates what is not-God within God" (p. 67)? Do such statements blur the sharp distinction between Creator and creation maintained by classical theism? Do they point in the direction of pantheism or atheism—as distinguished from what this book defends, panentheism or holism? What are the critical differences between theism, panentheism, pantheism, and atheism? Divide the class into four groups, each of which formulates and expounds the logic of one of these -isms. Let the class as a whole decide which is most persuasive.

11. Do you agree with the claim that Christ and the world are figures of God's creative-redemptive love at opposite ends of a continuum, each presupposing and completing the other? What does this claim imply about an understanding of both Christ and the world? What does it imply about the relationship of Jesus to other religious figures?

12. Take a few minutes to write down your own definition of *Spirit*. Compare what you have written with the approach taken in the text. What do you find strange, attractive, or both about the latter? Share your reflections with a neighbor.

13. The end of the chapter argues for a "pneumatocentric" as opposed to a "christocentric" model of the Trinity. What is at stake in these contrasting models? Suppose that your class or group is a church council charged with the responsibility of coming up with a new statement about the role of the Spirit in the life of God and the life of the world and about the relationship between Christ and the Spirit. What would you say?

14. How *do* God and the world interact?

4

Human Nature and Evil:
A Tragic Condition?

The Place of Humanity in Nature

To understand human nature, we must understand the whole of nature. We made a brief attempt to do so at the beginning of chapter 3. Human beings are not the product of a special act of creation but have emerged through a creative-evolutionary process that goes back billions of years, works through an interplay of random forces, and continues now for humans particularly in the form of intellectual and technological changes. We are biohistorical beings, products of biological and historical forces that have shaped us into what we are. Yet we are also spiritual beings, aware of who we are and of the greater whole of which we are a part. Such awareness has, from the earliest traces of human civilization, included a religious dimension, a sense of being related to and guided by the source of all that is.

Our ability to transcend nature tempts us to forget how deeply embedded we are in nature. Even the biblical story of creation, which ends by emphasizing the special relationship of human beings to God, begins by telling how God created the world: "In the beginning when God created the heavens and the earth, the earth was a formless void and darkness covered the face of the deep, while a wind from God swept over the face of the waters" (Gen. 1:1–2). A striking statement! Can we understand the void or the hidden deep that was apparently God's first work of creation as a mythic representation of the incredibly dense mass that exploded, according to the Big Bang theory, in the first instant of cosmic process? To be sure, the biblical story represents what physicists call the "infinite singularity" as infinite emptiness, whereas for science it is more like a place of zero volume and infinite density, but symbolically these have the same meaning: there is not yet any recognizable form or measure. This fluid and chaotic void or mass is the stuff God posits in order to have material with which to create, that is, to separate and define. It is the common origin of all that is, but it itself lacks determinate features.

Rather than thinking of chaos in negative terms as the nothingness or nonbeing to which Christian tradition has almost always consigned it, let us try thinking of it in positive terms as holding productive possibilities for creative development. According to recent scientific cosmologies, a fluid and formless *chaos* is one of the necessary conditions of creativity. Theologically we can say that chaos holds the potential for both good and evil, and the outcome is dependent on what God and we make of it. It is the condition of possibility for there being a world that is other than God, yet related to God. Chaos has the capacity for resistance: God and we have to struggle with it. Rather than a *creatio ex nihilo* (creation from nothing), what we find in the Bible, suggests Catherine Keller, is a *creatio ex profundis* (creation from the depths). We need not conclude that the chaotic depths represent an independent, antidivine matter. Although the biblical text is ambiguous about when the work of creation actually begins, theologically it is appropriate to affirm that chaos too comes from the sheer creative potency that God is. Notably, God works on the *face* of the deep or at the *edge* of chaos, as Keller observes. God does not control the depths, and what God creates is conditioned by the depths. The chaotic source introduces tragic conflicts as well as serendipitous confluences into the cosmos.

The creation story continues: "Then God said, 'Let there be light'; and there was light. . . . And God said, 'Let there be a dome in the midst of the waters, and let it separate the waters from the waters.' . . . And God said . . ." (Gen. 1:3 ff.). God speaks, and it happens: the divine imperative is an indicative. God's creative instrument is solely the word, not a common substance or a material causality. The word establishes the power and freedom of God, who is able to call into being merely by speaking, by using this most fragile, intangible, and seemingly powerless of instruments. At the same time, the word signifies that God is immanent in the world as the very power of being on which everything in the world directly depends: if God did not speak, it would not be. Of course, this is a metaphorical, not a literal speaking. The word (articulated breath) here represents the fluid, invisible, immense, and pervasive power of the Spirit of God, which sweeps like wind across the formless waters and sculpts them into a patterned cosmos.

The word creates by wresting form out of the formless, order from chaos. Word is what forms, shapes, configures. God's word shapes the formless cosmic matter into a *world*—a world of light and darkness, of heaven and earth, of waters and dry land, of vegetation and living creatures, of animals and humans, of man and woman. Forming and shaping are matters of distinguishing, separating, refining, reuniting. Here again there seems to be a striking consonance between the biblical myth and the scientific picture. According to the latter, following the beginning instant, the universe expanded into increasingly rich, diverse, and complex forms, and it continues to do so. From the initial chaos, order emerges through an ongoing creative process, but the chaotic element remains ever present. The biblical story, like scientific cosmologies, also depicts creation as a process that occurs not all at once but through time, although its time frame is couched in symbolic rather than literal numbers.

On the sixth day—the next-to-last day—God arrived at the creation of human beings.

> Then God said, "Let us make humankind [*'adham*] in our image, according to our likeness; and let them have dominion over the fish of the sea, and over the birds of the air, and over the cattle, and over all the wild animals of the earth, and over every creeping thing that creeps upon the earth."
> So God created humankind in his image,
> in the image of God he created them;
> male and female he created them. (Gen. 1:26–27)

In contrast to this elegant *Priestly account*, the Yahwist provides a rather more modest version: "Then the LORD God formed human being [*'adham*] from the dust of the ground, and breathed into his nostrils the breath of life; and human being became a living being" (Gen. 2:7, translation modified).

These two texts taken together mark the central themes of a *theological anthropology*. The *Yahwist's account* underscores the continuity of human beings with the rest of the world. *'Adham* was formed from the dust of the ground, *'adhamah*, and became a living being, a *nephesh*, through the inbreathing of the breath of life, *ruach*. The very name of human being, *'adham*, means "ground," but this ground is brought to life by the breath or Spirit of God. As an intelligent speaking being, *'adham* is essentially a *free* being. This is the central theme of the Priestly text. Freedom is defined in terms of certain constitutive relationships: the relationship to God, in whose image (as the utterly Free One) human beings are created; the relationship to the earth and its living creatures, over which *'adham* is to have "dominion"; and the relationship between man and woman as the primordial community in which human beings can be free for the other. Freedom is not an individualistic but a communal, relational concept for the Hebrew Bible. To be sure, these relationships are defined hierarchically and patriarchally, at least in the Priestly text. God has dominion over humans (yet they are God's truest image), humans over nature (although dominion carries with it stewardship), and man over woman (although they are created as equals and partners). Today we must develop a concept of freedom that affirms the repressed intuitions of the ancient text, replacing hierarchy with equality and dominion with reciprocity and mutual responsibility.

Human beings are free primarily by virtue of their capacity to speak: language is the road to freedom. This is reflected in the biblical story of origins. God creates by calling into being; God communicates with *'adham* by means of spoken commands; *'adham* is given the capacity of naming the animals; the man and the woman speak to each other; and the subtle speech of the serpent is the instrument of deception. The linguistic ability of human beings sets them off from other living beings, but not absolutely. The most intelligent species of animals communicate in signs that approximate language in remarkable ways, and they exhibit a playfulness that approximates what we call freedom. Recent experiments suggest that these animals possess some form of self-consciousness and experience emotions.

The ability to learn and use a language is principally a function of brain capacity and the possession of vocal organs for articulated speech. The evolution of these capacities required millions of years and occurred in imperceptibly small steps. Still, with the arrival of fully developed language along with the freedom, self-consciousness, cognitive processes, and aesthetic awareness that language makes possible, we have the sense of a threshold crossing to a new dimension of life that we call "human." Human being is the first truly liberated being in creation. It is appropriate, therefore, to designate our species not only as *Homo sapiens* (wise humanity) but also as *Homo verbum* (verbal humanity) and *Homo liber* (free humanity). Intelligence enables language, which elicits freedom. It is above all as *Homo liber* that human being is the *imago Dei*. There is also a feedback effect: freedom purifies language, which strengthens intelligence.

The biblical story assumes that the creation of human beings is the purpose and goal of the whole creative process. A similar assumption is made by the so-called anthropic principle defended by some present-day cosmologists. In its strongest form, it holds that the very nature of the physical universe makes the emergence of life and the evolution of intelligent observers in it not only possible but inevitable. Whether or not we accept this principle, it is evident that, if a tendency of the cosmos is to produce complexity, then by far the greatest complexity we know is we ourselves. Ian Barbour puts it this way: "There are a hundred trillion synapses in a human brain; the number of possible ways of connecting them is greater than the number of atoms in the universe. A higher level of organization and a greater richness of experience occurs in a human being than in a thousand lifeless galaxies." We should not, however, confuse this complexity with the goal or the center of cosmic process. Barbour goes on to point out: "The chemical elements in your hand and in your brain were forged in the furnaces of the stars. The cosmos is all of a piece. It is multileveled; each new higher level was built on lower levels from the past. Humanity is the most advanced form of life we know, but it is fully a part of a wider process in space and time."

The theory of evolution underscores both the connection and the uniqueness of human beings vis-à-vis the wider process, and it leaves open the question of purpose. We are formed of cosmic dust—almost literally, through random variations in the genetic code combined with a process of natural selection (both competitive and cooperative) by which species emerge. Humans and apes are descended from common ancestors going back 4 to 6 million years. Recent discoveries have established that the earliest known hominids, who walked upright on two legs, are at least 4 million years old. The first forms of the human species, *Homo habilis*, who made and used tools, were present about 2.5 million years ago in Africa. Somewhere between 2 million and 1 million years ago came a dramatic growth of the brain and with it the appearance of archaic forms of *Homo sapiens*. A deviant branch, the Neanderthals, were in Europe 100,000 years ago, followed by the first modern *Homo sapiens*, some 12,000 to 40,000 years ago. They possessed language and made significant contributions in arts, crafts, tools, and other skills of early culture, as evidenced by their cave paintings, artifacts, and burial rituals. During the Neolithic period (10,000–3000 B.C.E.), the pace of change quickened, with the taming of animals, the development of agriculture, the invention of writing (Sumerian inscriptions, about 4000 B.C.E.), and the beginning of the great civilizations in Mesopotamia, Egypt, and India. With writing, new possibilities ramified in an astonishingly rapid and ever-accelerating process, which has brought us today to the age of information technology. We know more than ever before, but there is little evidence that *Homo sapiens* is evolving into a truly *wiser* species.

As we look back, we are filled with awe. An extreme fine-tuning was required for the process to have turned out as it did. Minute changes in the physical constants would have resulted in an uninhabitable universe. Some interpreters have argued that chance mutation and natural selection alone are not enough to account for the evolution of highly adapted organisms, and they point out that the odds against human evolution are extremely high, especially in the limited time span in which it occurred. Others such as Gordon Kaufman have suggested that a *serendipitous creativity* is at work in the world. Cosmic process has produced more than would have been expected, more than seemed possible, moving irreversibly, through diverse trajectories, toward more complex forms, toward what we call "history" and "spirit." This cannot be attributed to chance alone. Rather, says Kaufman, there seems to be a tendency in the ultimate nature or mystery of things toward the production of ever higher and richer, centered forms of being. Is this proof of divine creativity or even of a divine creator? No, there is no such scientific proof. Yet the belief that God really did form human beings "from dust" and "in the image of God"—not instantly but through an amazing evolutionary process—is not incompatible with what we know today from scientific observation.

(Before reading the next two sections, take the quiz found in exercise 5 at the end of the chapter.)

Imago Dei: **Human Being as Embodied Freedom**

If freedom is the image of God in humanity, then freedom must be a central theme of theological anthropology. Yet human beings are also natural, material beings, formed of cosmic dust. These two aspects—freedom and nature—constitute the fundamental mystery and dilemma of human existence. Human freedom is an *embodied freedom*—a freedom limited by and reciprocal with the body, our individual bodies as well as the body politic and the whole body of nature. Ours is an incarnate, contingent, finite freedom, yet still a freedom. With respect to our individual responsibility and action, we are determined, limited, moved by our interests and motives as well as by our physical needs, desires, and capabilities. With respect to interpersonal and social relationships, we depend on a structure of intersubjectivity and a social world that are always already given. With respect to our material embodiment, we are determined and strictly limited by the fundamental necessities of the human condition: the contingencies of birth and of genetic and psychic endowment, the role of the unconscious, the processes of growth and adaptation, and the finality of death. Despite all of this, our freedom is not obliterated but constrained, rendered fragile yet tenacious, vulnerable to destruction but capable of being restored.

Human beings are not simple entities but complex networks of relationships. I propose that we think of these as relationships of freedom, of which four can be distinguished: *personal, interpersonal, social, and transpersonal.* It is these that constitute human beings as "selves." A self is not a pre-existent substance but something that comes into being and is ever-modified by its relationships to itself, to communities of persons, to the social world, to the natural environment, and to the ultimate mystery of things. The last of these relationships—transpersonal freedom or openness to transcendence—appears in and through the others. I direct special attention to it.

Personal, Interpersonal, and Social Freedom

Our *personal being* is elusive because it is so immediate to us. We intuitively know ourselves to be subjects or agents engaged in decisions and actions for which we can assume responsibility. This is the most elemental form of freedom: self-knowing, presence-to-self. We catch sight of ourselves in the process of choosing and acting. We avail ourselves of resources provided by the past and by our environment, and we can project or intend new possibilities for the future through decisions and actions taken in the present. In this way, we achieve an integration of time and are not captive to its mere succession any more than we are to our physical environment. We have an identity that is not simply given by something other than ourselves.

At the same time, we know ourselves to be embodied, biological beings who are an integral part of the natural world. We know that we are motivated by powerful biological drives and instincts and that we are limited by our bodily capabilities. We are unable to return literally to the past or to leap ahead into the future or to be in more than one physical location at any given moment. We are subject to the fundamental necessities of finite physical existence. Yet we sense that we need not be trapped by these things. Motives become causal factors in the freedom of decision, and they can *incline without compelling us*, as Paul Ricoeur suggested. Bodily capabilities and limits challenge us to new heights of achievement, and we can extend these capabilities almost indefinitely through tools and instruments. We do not simply live and die but transfuse this simple facticity with a complex network of meanings, purposes, desires, passions. Yet it is tempting to surrender to the *involuntary*, to abandon the human project; we often lack courage and give in to debilitating fears.

We know that we are not alone in the world and that we exist in *interpersonal relationships*. There are others like ourselves, others in whom we see ourselves reflected, others whom we must *recognize* to be other and whose experience we can never immediately experience ourselves. This strange elusiveness of the other constitutes the fact of *alterity*, which is the precondition of all genuine relationships. Emmanuel Levinas refers to it as the "face," "the infinitely strange and mysterious presence of something which contests my projected meanings of it." The face of the other makes claims on us, claims of both compassion and obligation. When we provide compassion and sympathy for one another and meet the needs of one another in a relationship of mutuality and inclusion, then we experience freedom in the realm of the interpersonal. Freedom means not only presence to oneself but also presence with and for others; it means to exist as "spirit" as well as "self." Human beings possess the possibility for an authentic communion of free and equal persons, in which is found a mutuality of recognition and an intending of the other for the sake of the other. Yet there is also the possibility for intense conflict, suffering, and alienation.

Interpersonal freedom does not occur in a vacuum but in the framework of well-established social structures and processes. These consist of a legacy of customs, laws, values, and roles, which are borne by such vehicles as language, belief systems, institutions, cultural practices, and rituals. If such things did not already exist, there could be no interpersonal relationships and not even any personal agency. *Social freedom* consists fundamentally in *just* systems, practices, and values. The goal of society is to create a commonwealth of freedom and justice in which human beings can dwell humanly, a liberated and liberating sociopolitical-economic structure. Hegel designated the latter as a system of "right" or "justice," and he envisioned it metaphorically as "the kingdom of freedom actualized, the world of spirit brought forth out of itself like a second nature"—an expression that is reminiscent not only of Jesus' proclamation of the kingdom of God but also of Aristotle's definition of the *polis* as the "community of the free." Of course, justice is accomplished only partially and fragmentarily under the conditions of historical existence. Nowhere is the fragility of human freedom more tragically evident than in the realm of the social.

If the world of spirit, the social world, is humanity's "second nature," then our "first nature" is precisely the natural world. Nature is the ultimate alterity of human being, a difference that can never be reduced to the same, the identity of the self. Yet we dwell in the natural world and depend on it for the actualization of our humanity. Nature enters into the constitution of human being not only through the social world, which represents simply the construction of the system of nature into a human dwelling place, but also through our individual embodiments and through the fundamental necessities of life on this planet.

Transpersonal Freedom: Openness to Transcendence

Some theological and most philosophical anthropologies limit themselves to the first three relationships just described. I believe it necessary, however, to add a fourth dimension, transpersonal freedom, which is the ground and goal of all other forms of human freedom—personal, interpersonal, and social—even though it is not separable from them and appears only in and through them. The relationship to transcendence does not come into existence only in concrete experiences of redemption. It is already there as a structural possibility for all human beings: it is the *imago Dei* in humanity. If humans are *fallible* in consequence of their fragility and vulnerability, as I argue in the next section, then they must also be *redeemable*; otherwise the human condition would be purely and solely tragic. This claim is theological, but evidence for it appears in the way human beings exist in the world, namely, as *free* despite their finitude, fragility, vulnerabilities, and fallenness.

Somehow, finite, embodied human freedom sustains itself in the face of the overwhelming and seductive power of the involuntary. My thesis is that it remains a viable possibility in the context of the organic and social necessities of life only if persons are *open* to a liberating power that transcends all their physical and social environments and redeems them from a self-imposed bondage. It is a peculiarity of human beings that they remain open into the beyond, the infinite, the eternal horizon. No other living creature demonstrates this characteristic, and it is this that makes us religious beings. Human needs and instincts are not in themselves infinite; only when they are traversed by language do they become desires, quests, passions, intrinsically unfulfillable. No matter how frequently we are positively reinforced, we remain dissatisfied, unfulfilled, incapable of attaining a final happiness. Saint Augustine in the *Confessions* recognized the infinitude of human openness: our hearts are restless, he said, until they find their rest in God.

Openness is the key relationship in a theological anthropology. It is the foundation of the responsible action that makes up personal freedom, of the communion that creates interpersonal freedom, and of the just practices and values that characterize social freedom, for it alone provides the context in which freedom can survive and flourish. Openness not only relativizes all finite goods but also makes us receptive to God's self-communication. It enables us to read the signs of God's presence in nature and history. It appears as hope for the coming of God's kingdom. It gives us courage to risk our being in the perils and adventures of existence. It implies faith in God as the One who fills the transcendent horizon, for God's power and project alone provide the true home of freedom. The opposite of hope is despair, which before God is sin. The opposite of faith is unbelief or broken faith, which is at the heart of idolatry. The opposite of courage is fear, which is at the heart of flight. Without courage, faith, and hope, we fall into a debilitating alienation from self, other selves, and world.

If human beings are open to transcendence, then they are open to the possibility of redemption; they are *redeemable*. Are redemption and liberating power *realities* as opposed to mere possibilities? Are human beings not simply redeemable but actually redeemed? The answers to these questions require moving beyond an analysis of basic structures of freedom to a community of faith with its symbols of bondage and liberation. If redemption were only a possibility and not also an actuality—if nothing comes forth in the open but emptiness and absurdity—then human existence would have no orientation and meaning. If the vision of a home of freedom were simply an illusion, then all such religious visions, indeed religion as such, would have to be rejected as a false form of consciousness, a wish fulfillment—as has been claimed by great critics of religion like Feuerbach, Marx, Nietzsche, Freud.

Yet the fact that human beings really do have courage and hope, really do play and love, and do so soberly and without illusions suggests that the reality of redemption has already inscribed itself on the structural possibilities of human existence and is discernible there before and apart from an explicit theology of redemption, a Christology and *pneumatology*. The inscription, however, remains ambiguous and obscure, subject to varying interpretations. To construe it as a structure of openness to transcendence is a theological act. Theological anthropology presupposes a relationship to a redemptive God. Thus it cannot be the foundation on which everything is built but is part of a circle of interpretation in which each element presupposes and founds every other element.

Tragedy: From Fragility to Sin

The fact that human beings are not only fallible but faulty seems to have an empirical certainty that is lacking in comparable claims about redeemability and redemption. Yet to construe the human condition as tragic and sinful also entails a theological act. We are fragile beings, subject to a peculiar instability in the synthesis of finitude and freedom that make up human existence—the tendency of these elements to pull in opposite and mutually destructive directions. On one hand, we tend to draw everything into the autonomous self and to make other persons functions of our own agendas, thus violating otherness by reducing it to the same, rupturing and destroying community, and turning the social world into a system of domination and *alienation*. There seems to be a primordial egoism or narcissism at the heart of the human being. On the other hand, we tend to expand bodily needs and desires far beyond what we actually require to exist and to absolutize death as the final and inescapable necessity of finite existence. There seems to be a primordial, fatal attraction to the involuntary at the heart of human being, an abandoning of the human project, a death wish.

These tendencies reflect the tragedy of the human condition. The tragic, writes Edward Farley, "refers to a situation in which the conditions of well-being require and are interdependent with situations of limitation, frustration, challenge, and suffering." The tragic shows itself in the form of distinctive vulnerabilities that adhere to the various spheres of human freedom—personal, interpersonal, social, transpersonal. Because our personal being is threatened by temporal, social, and biological limits, we must struggle to survive and in the process develop aggressive tendencies. Because interpersonal relationships can become so intense, intimate, and fulfilling, they are also subject to intense suffering when they are damaged or cease to exist. Wounding and thus alienation are inevitable, says Farley, because "at the heart of the interhuman is a vast set of incompatibilities that originate in the irreducible otherness of the participants."

These incompatibilities also appear in the social world in conflicts among group interests, competitions for resources or living space, and cultural strategies of repression for the sake of order—all of which lead to widespread social suffering. In the realm of the transpersonal, we face the possibility that the ultimate horizon of our existence is empty and that death is our final and only fate. We become preoccupied with death, both fearing and venerating it; it becomes our god, corroding courage and faith, shutting us off from the true and holy God. The anxiety that drives us to sin has its roots in all of these vulnerabilities.

Why did God create us as fragile beings with these tragic vulnerabilities? Is there an evil or demonic or destructive dimension within divinity itself? Were we created from chaotic material that God could only partially subdue? Are the disproportion between freedom and finitude and the tragic vulnerabilities of life endemic to the very project of creating free beings distinct from God, that is, finite beings? This last idea has prevailed in the Jewish and Christian traditions, but it is not without problems. Does it mean that God is subject to certain logical or *ontological* constraints in the work of creation? Does God limit godself, "withdraw," as *kabalistic* teaching suggests, to make space for a world that is other than God? Does God allow evil for the sake of, or as an instrument of, a greater good such as redemption? If human beings were created as fragile and vulnerable, must they assume sole or primary responsibility for sin?

The only religiously satisfying answer to these questions is that of a God who takes the cosmic and human tragedy on and into godself, thereby both completing and overcoming tragedy. This is the meaning of the redemptive suffering of the cross, a suffering undergone by God in Christ. God is not exempt from the tragic condition of the world—which as a condition for the possibility of good also allows for the possibility of evil—but shares, suffers, and redeems it.

Just as there is a mystery to the presence of tragedy, of susceptibility to sin, which cannot be fully grasped, so also the transition from the possibility of sin and evil to their actuality—the transition from fallibility to fault—cannot be directly described. We are faced with the paradox to which Reinhold Niebuhr called attention, namely, that sin seems to be inevitable but not necessary. Why and how is it that human beings freely bring about their own bondage to sin?

The Bible does not offer an explanation but tells a story, the story of the *fall* of humanity in the third chapter of Genesis. The plot of this story is woven around the theme of *deception*. The serpent, we are told, "was more crafty than any other wild animal that the LORD God had made" (Gen. 3:1). The deceit was in the falsehood that the creature, without penalty to itself, could become its own creator, its own God. "You will be like God, knowing good and evil" (3:5): a distortion of the truth that human being is created in the image of God and that knowledge and freedom are what constitute the image of God in humanity. Hence it is not an outright falsehood but one that conceals the truth. An out-and-out lie would be easier to detect and resist. Knowledge and freedom *are* what make us "like God," but they are a finite knowledge and freedom. The ensuing punishments (Gen. 3:14–19) are reminders of our finitude, our earthly nature (pain in childbearing, the toil and sweat of labor, death as return to the ground from which we were taken). The prohibition against eating from the tree of immortality is what constitutes the *difference* between divinity and humanity. The question about the prohibition, which the serpent cunningly exaggerates ("Did God say, 'You shall not eat from *any* tree in the garden'?"), arouses the human desire for infinity—the "evil infinite"—which perverts the finitude of freedom, tempting us to transgress our bodily limits.

Human self-deceit is symbolized by the serpent because it is experienced as a seduction from without. "The serpent," wrote Paul Ricoeur, "would be a part of ourselves which we do not recognize; he would be the seduction of ourselves by ourselves, projected into the seductive object." The remarkable thing about deceit is that it deceives itself, forgets itself, falls prey to the illusion that someone else is to blame. The victimizer blames the victim, the man blames the woman, the woman blames the serpent. We humans are in fact responsible for self-deception and the acts of sin that follow it, but as individuals we are not absolutely responsible. Sin and evil are always already there in the social environment in which we find ourselves. The serpent, Ricoeur continued, "represents the aspect of evil that could not be absorbed into the responsible freedom of human beings." This antecedent evil constitutes a situation of temptation to which individuals yield in virtue of their weakness, anxiety, and desire. There is no ultimate explanation of *why* individuals yield. They just always do, deceiving themselves in the process, blaming others, forgetting what they already know, weaving the social net in which they are trapped all the tighter. Because of the self-reinforcing character of deception, once sin occurs it is impossible to break its grip from inside the condition of sin itself. Saint Augustine remarked that by sinning we lose the capacity not to sin (*non posse non peccare*).

Sin entails a disruption of the personal and interpersonal structures of human being. These disruptions—to be identified as idolatry, flight, and alienation—correspond to specific features of the tragic vulnerability that attends finite freedom. They are rooted in a primordial brokenness of faith; they are driven by debilitating fears that arise from the anxiety-producing fragility of the human condition; and they issue in a *bondage of the will* that stifles the freedom at the heart of human being. This bondage, in turn, acquires certain cosmic and social objectifications that demonically intensify sin, converting it into structures of evil that correspond to the structures of sin. Pauline categories are helpful at this point: *law* as a symbol of the constraints of civilization entails an objectification of alienation; "death" not as physical mortality but as a binding cosmic force represents an objectification of flight; and "worldly powers" objectify idolatry in the form of ideologies and injustice.

Such at least is my thesis, and it has three implications for viewing the connection between sin and evil: (1) No genuine liberation or salvation is attained simply by removing the objective conditions of alienation, death, ideologies, and injustice. The powers that enthrall humanity are not simply external to the psyche but internal to it. (2) The cosmic and social objectifications of bondage *do* reinforce and demonically intensify personal and interpersonal acts of sin. Hence no genuine liberation or salvation leaves these objectifications untouched. Psyche is not reducible to society, or society to psyche. (3) Because deception deceives and forgets itself and because freedom binds itself, liberation is impossible through knowledge alone or self-emancipation alone. What is required is *saving* knowledge, a revelation, a redemptive deliverance, a divine reshaping of broken and distorted relationships. This reshaping might be thought of as the work of God's *Wisdom*, which counteracts human deception and foolishness.

Idolatry (Broken Faith)

Why call sin *idolatry*? Because in the first instance it is a relationship to God that is broken or distorted in some way. The Hebrew Bible identified sin as the rupturing of a covenant relationship with God and the setting up of ourselves as gods. The Apostle Paul used various terms to express the idea of sin as rebellion, pride, disobedience. It is not a matter of disobeying a divine autocrat who demands submission from human beings. Instead, human beings strive to make their condition secure through attachment to false foundations and mundane goods— a securing that takes the form of material possessions, economic security, erotic pleasures, political ideologies, religious belief-systems. Sin, in Edward Farley's words, arises from "a skewed passion for the eternal"; it represents a "mundanizing of the eternal horizon." It is a substitution of finite gods or idols for the true and holy God. It is a refusal to believe that God alone is the source of our strength and salvation. It is, in other words, a primordial act of unbelief, which according to Paul Tillich lies at the root of all particular forms of sin. It is, in H. Richard Niebuhr's eloquent expression, "broken faith," a pervasive distrust that appears in the form of hostility, fear, and isolation.

For most of us, idolatrous unbelief assumes the form not of a Promethean defiance of the divinities but of domination over our fellow human beings. If we set up ourselves, our goods and interests, as gods in place of God, we tend to draw everything into our domain and make it subservient to our desires. Thus idolatry issues above all in the distortion and destruction of *interhuman* relationships. God appears in the picture not primarily as the object or victim of sin and certainly not as the author of sin, but rather as the provider of resources for combating sin and evil. God is damaged by sin not directly but indirectly, through the damage humans suffer; for God puts godself at risk in the world and is wounded by the terrible wounds humans inflict on one another. We sin against God not principally by breaking a divine prohibition, as the biblical story of the fall and much of the theological tradition puts it, thereby creating a legalistic and punitive framework for interpreting sin. We do so by violating a relationship of trust not only with God but with our fellow creatures; thus Adam and Eve, knowing their nakedness, hid from God, passed the blame to each other, and inaugurated conflict and violence.

Flight (Fear)

If idolatry is the "sin of infinitude," the "faulty infinite" of freedom by which humans defy or deny the finite limits of their existence and seek to become Godlike, then, as Søren Kierkegaard suggested, there must exist another basic form of sin, the diametrical opposite of the first, yet profoundly related to it: the sin of finitude, the denial of life and freedom, the apotheosis of death. Such a form of sin is known in the Bible, and it can be described as *flight*, sloth, failure, despair, surrender, submission. Surrender and submission come into play when the second form of sin is viewed in terms of interhuman rather than divine-human relationships Acquiescence in or accommodation to the domination of another, or subjection in the face of abuse, is a form of sin—perhaps the form of sin most commonly experienced by women and minorities. This point is difficult to acknowledge, because responsibility for victimization rests with the victimizer, not the victim. If the victim has the option of resisting rather than collaborating, however, then the latter is a form of flight. Survival is of course a fundamental human drive, but one must learn to survive by resisting, not by surrendering; otherwise one survives only to undergo an inward death.

Flight is perhaps the primary form of sin in our time, one of whose symptoms is the widespread use of drugs, alcohol, and other opiates as a means of escape from reality. Not only flight but also idolatry seem to be rooted in a fundamental and pervasive fear—fear of vulnerability, otherness, difference, change, life itself, and ultimately death. The fear manifests itself in aggressive, repressive, and submissive attitudes. There surely is a connection between anxiety (an ontological condition of embodied freedom) and fear (the concrete phobias that rob our lives of meaning), but it is difficult to establish a direct causal link between them. Vis-à-vis God, anxiety falsely interpreted takes the form of idolatry; vis-à-vis the world, it takes the form of fear. Fear is the emotion that drives human beings to the most terrible of deeds. The world that God loves is converted into a field of hatreds, a killing field.

Alienation (Violation)

Idolatry and flight are closely related forms of primarily personal sin, although each has interhuman implications and each is objectified in cosmic and social powers. There is in addition a form of sin characteristic of interpersonal relationships, namely, *alienation–malignant* alienation, as distinct from the benign alienation that accompanies the incompatibilities intrinsic to interpersonal relationships. Alienation becomes malignant (sinful) when relations are poisoned by violation, victimization, or both. (At this point I am helped by the work of both Edward Farley and Wendy Farley.)

The violation of a relationship fundamentally alters its nature. Individuals involved in a violative relationship use the elements of the relationship against each other in destructive ways. This is evident in abusive marital, sexual, or parent-child relationships, as well as in patterns of sexual harassment and in situations of manipulation, control, and deception. In fact, all relationships of inequality are potentially violative and thus alienating. They breed attitudes of resentment in the violated and guilt in the violator. Guilt arises from the awareness that the relationships have been damaged and that the damage cannot be repaired without building a new relationship. Yet individuals find themselves trapped in destructive relationships, unable to attain a basis for rebuilding. The fact of violating and having been violated remains as a stain that cannot be washed away or a wound that does not heal. The feelings of guilt thus aroused are internalized by individuals and spread into the social world, where they infect institutional and legal relationships.

Bondage of the Will (Conscience)

Guilt, according to Paul Ricoeur, expresses "the paradox toward which the idea of fault points—namely, the concept of a human being who is responsible *and* captive, or rather a being who is responsible for being captive—in short the concept of the *servile will*." Guilt is the "achieved internality of sin"; it is the subjective awareness of the objective situation of sin; it is sin raised to the level of moral consciousness or "conscience." We *know* that we are responsible for acts of idolatry, flight, and alienation, and this very knowledge has a binding effect. We are bound by the knowledge that we are responsible, bound by self-blame (knowing that we can no longer blame the other). We resort to various indirect ways of talking about this, using symbolisms of captivity such as flesh, infection, defilement, possession, because, in the words of Ricoeur, "the paradox of a captive free will—the paradox of a *servile will*—is insupportable for thought. That freedom must be delivered and that this deliverance is deliverance from self-enslavement cannot be said directly; yet it is the central theme of 'salvation.'"

Injustice: From Sin to Evil

The fact that personal and interpersonal sin issues in a bondage of the will means that sin has the capacity not only to alter the structures of the self but also to assume its own objective power over individual persons and interpersonal relationships. The objectification of sin appears in the alteration of certain cosmic and social structures, which in turn profoundly affect individual and communal selves. I refer to this alteration as *evil*. The distinction between sin and evil is tenuous; some theologians use the terms synonymously. However, I find it helpful to think of evil as not merely a consequence that follows on sin but as a dynamic that magnifies and reinforces it, converting it into something that cannot be remedied by a change of heart. Evil is a consequence that also precedes individual acts of sin; it becomes embedded in the historical destiny that tempts us to sin, thus adding a tragic dimension to moral responsibility.

Two basic forms of evil may be identified by using categories suggested by the Apostle Paul. Death (in the sense of *thanatos*) is primarily a cosmic objectification of sin because it alters our way of being in the world as natural beings. Law and the worldly powers are primarily social objectifications, issuing in institutionalized alienation, ideologies, and above all injustice.

Cosmic Evil: Death

Death is the ultimate form of human bondage, infusing all the other forms. But what do we mean by "death"? Death in the sense of mortality, physical perishing, is simply an aspect of our finitude, our bodily existence, something that happens to all of us in the course of nature. Yet physical mortality takes on the aspect of a binding power when it becomes an object of over-riding anxiety and an occasion for flight from life, freedom, and responsibility. When this happens, death becomes what Paul in Romans and 1 Corinthians calls *thanatos*, a binding, deadly power, the "enemy," and as such an objectification of the sin of flight. We are vulnerable to this transposition of mortality into death because we have come to believe that mortality means the end of the unique and irreplaceable individuals that we are: we are threatened by a fear of extinction.

Mortality is the enemy only if it is *not* the case that God is the victor over mortal death, preserving but also transforming each individual in God's life-giving presence, subsuming our personal identity in a way we cannot grasp. Not to believe that God is the victor is to live according to the flesh, to venerate the flesh (or mortality) as a god. In that instant, mortality becomes for us death proper, *thanatos*, a deadly, evil power that flows from sin—both the sin of idolatry or unbelief and the sin of flight or fear. "The wages of sin is death" (Rom. 6:23): this formulation should not be taken in the sense that death is the punishment for sin, but rather that death is the fruit of sin (compare Gal. 6:8), the "sickness" (Kierkegaard's term) that results from sin. When mortality becomes death in this uniquely Pauline sense, it becomes a binding, evil power (Rom. 6:21–22; 8:2, 21). The thing that enslaves or captures us above all else is our own mortality converted into death. Once this conversion occurs, we are more likely to impose death on others or to justify killing—the most violent form of injustice. Death becomes a god that fatally attracts us.

The only basis for not living according to the flesh is to believe that it is possible to live according to another power, which is the power of God or the Spirit. To have faith in God is to know that mortality is not the ultimate power that cuts us off from God and life. It is to know that *thanatos* as such is an illusion—a deadly illusion, to be sure—and that the truth is not death alone but resurrection from the dead. Resurrection does not cancel or deny mortality; it accepts it, assumes it, preserves and transforms it. Mortality or perishability becomes a differentiating moment in the life of God. Then it is no longer capable of being converted into *thanatos*, and in this sense the power of death (its "victory" or "sting") is destroyed. In the process we too are "changed," we "put on" immortality (1 Cor. 15:50–54) in the sense that the basis for our personal identity is no longer our mortal bodies but the eternal, differentiated unity of God. This idea is further considered in chapters 5 and 6.

Is death a problem that afflicts only human beings, or is there also a death of nature? Paul does assert that the whole of creation was subjected to "futility," to "bondage to decay" (Rom. 8:20–21). This decay is not a consequence of sin (with the important exception that humans inflict damage on nature through their arrogant disregard of its balances) but of dynamisms at work in nature itself. There appears to be a drift toward futility in nature, a waywardness, an undertow toward disintegration and destructiveness. The scientific term for this phenomenon is *entropy*. On one hand, energy gradually changes into less useful and differentiated forms. On the other hand, the thrust toward differentiation in nature, which is necessary to the evolutionary process, tends to over-reach itself, to migrate into rivalry and violence, to increase disorder, to move toward death rather than life. The struggle for life becomes excessive, goes beyond what is actually necessary for survival; this can be seen in cancerous growth and in gratuitous violence among animals. Natural systems often interact destructively, such as volcanic eruptions, earthquakes, floods, tornadoes, hurricanes, climatic changes, and asteroid impacts, all of which destroy existing forms of life.

These phenomena may belong to the condition of possibility of there being a created world at all. In that sense, the condition of nature is tragic, not evil, but it has evil consequences for the living beings that suffer from and in the process. Life is destroyed for the sake of life, and death seems to stalk the cosmos.

Social Evil: Injustice

By *injustice*, I mean the disruption, distortion, or destruction of just or right relationships. Right relationships are defined by the relationships of freedom that are fundamentally constitutive of the human person. The injustice that accrues on the disruption of these relationships can be understood as an objectification of the first and third forms of sin that I have sought to identify, namely, idolatry and alienation. (Death is an objectification of the second form, flight.) Acts of sin become embedded in social, cultural, and political practices, taking on the character of law and worldly powers.

Law is a highly complex and ambiguous reality. It is obviously necessary for any ordered and just society because it limits political power and establishes rules for fair and consistent practices. Yet it can also become an instrument of suppression and control. For the Hebrew

Bible, law (*torah*) is the revelation of the right way of life for the people of God. It functions more as teaching than as regulation, but it can assume an oppressive quality if it is codified in a system of rules that must be obeyed for the sake of salvation, or if it serves as an instrument for heightening the consciousness of guilt. In this case, law itself becomes, to use Pauline language, one of the primary objectifications of bondage, a "law of sin and of death" (Rom. 8:2).

The form in which law in the binding sense appears in the social world is principally that of alienation, which pervades all levels of corporate life. The patriarchalism that has for millennia characterized most societies, Western and Eastern, is a form of institutionalized alienation, the perpetual violation of women as subjects. The rules that accompany modern bureaucracies (states, agencies, legal systems, corporations, universities, churches, marketplaces) are intrinsically alienating because they treat persons as units of an impersonal process rather than as individual subjects, and they convert relationships of equality into ones based on power and wealth. Economic and market systems rely to a significant degree on manipulation and depersonalization.

The positive function of law as the precondition of freedom in a constitutional democracy can be inverted into its opposite: the slogan "law and order" serves as code language for oppression when dominant power groups are threatened by resistance. Law can be readily manipulated to our advantage and an opponent's disadvantage. Fascist, totalitarian, and communist regimes are highly legalistic; in most capitalist democracies, the systemic controls are more subtle and humane but no less real. Thus law is an ambiguous reality in our corporate lives—necessary to social existence yet a ready seat for social evil.

The *worldly powers* to which Paul refers in Romans and 1 Corinthians can be viewed as objectifications of the sin of idolatry in various social evils. Paul speaks both of "spirit powers," which have their domain in "heaven," and of "earthly powers." The former is clearly a mythological conception—the idea that God rules the world through angels or elemental spirits, which have fallen and become destructive as a consequence of the general rebellion of the creation against the Creator.

I propose to think of these spirit powers in a nonmythological way as *ideologies*, that is, as rationalizations of unjust practices by means of uncritical beliefs that often have an emotional or irrational basis. (*Ideology* can also be used in a more neutral sociological sense to refer to the way in which theories and ideas contribute to social practices. I use the term in its more common negative sense.) Like the personal sin of which they are an objectification, ideologies are driven by deeply seated fears, and they obscure or mask the true reasons for believing and behaving in certain ways. They represent a form of self-delusion as well as public deception.

The -isms and phobias that concern us today are all ideologies in this sense. Racism, sexism, classism, and naturism all have a common structure: they rationalize an unjust practice (slavery, patriarchy, social stratification, environmental exploitation) by asserting the inherent inferiority of dark-skinned peoples, of women, of classes associated with physical labor, of nature as something rightly subjugated by humans; and by claiming that such relationships of inequality belong to the "natural law" willed by God. *Homophobia* and xenophobia likewise have a common structure: the fear of sexual orientations or of ethnic groups different from the orientations and groups with which we ourselves are associated. The unfamiliar is judged to be wrong or threatening, and biblical prejudices toward the other are elevated into divine laws. Our enemies become God's enemies, and conflict with the other takes on the aspect of a holy war. Fear even more than idolatry, or in combination with idolatry, drives this form of injustice.

Paul was less interested in the earthly powers, the so-called rulers of this age, for he thought they would soon pass away with the return of Christ. As a consequence, he took what appear to us to be compromising stands on the most sensitive political issues of his day: the hegemony of Rome, the institution of slavery, and the subordination of women. Paul's successors, including ourselves, have had to accept the reality that the eschaton will not come soon, and that the world in which we live has inherited a heavy and unrelenting legacy of unjust practices—political, social, economic, cultural, and environmental. These are connected to their legitimating ideologies but represent harm and suffering imposed on individuals and groups. Racism results in slavery, apartheid, prejudice; sexism in patriarchalism and the subordination of women; homophobia in the suppression and victimization of gays, lesbians, and bisexuals; classism in a system of stratification that withholds access to wealth and creates poverty; *ethnocentrism* in cultural conflict and domination; xenophobia in war.

To these must be added the exploitation of nature and the recognition that social justice and ecojustice are intertwined.

The ideologies and practices of injustice have a common characteristic: they withhold from an entity that which is necessary for its flourishing or well-being. Justice, by contrast, means to give to each being what belongs to it or is due to it for the sake of its perfection. This is the definition of justice proposed by Thomas Aquinas, who observed further that God is supremely just and also supremely liberal in justice, for God gives not for the sake of some benefit expected from the giving, but simply because of the goodness and befittingness of the giving. Humans for the most part are supremely selfish, withholding what is needed for the well-being of the other.

These practices of injustice and oppression are the most terrible forms of human evil because they are so destructive, so widespread, so distant from what we ordinarily think of as personal sin. They spread a mantle of hatred and hostility over the world God created for the sake of love. We find ourselves hopelessly entangled in this mantle, in bondage to the interlocking dynamic of sin and evil. No finite power can break the logic of self-securing and its demonic intensifications. We cannot save ourselves. What is needed is a new incarnation of God's love, powerful enough to break the grip of sin and death, to reconcile alienated groups, to set us free from destructive practices, to proclaim the kingdom of justice.

EXERCISES

1. Discuss some of the similarities and dissimilarities between the biblical story of creation and recent scientific accounts of origins. Which seem more significant to you, the similarities or the differences?

2. Stage a debate between creationist and evolutionary versions of the origin of humanity. Which is more persuasive in terms of (a) scriptural authority, (b) religious intuition, and (c) scientific evidence?

3. This chapter argues that chaos plays an important role in the process of creation: chaos introduces both "tragic conflicts" and "serendipitous confluences" into the cosmos. What does this mean, and do you agree with it? Look at one of the recent books

on chaos theory, and ask yourself how chaos might be part of the divine creativity.

4. Read the first two chapters of Genesis aloud in class. Assign a different reader for each set of verses. Pause where the paragraph breaks occur in the English text, and discuss the meaning of what has just been read.

5. Take this true-false quiz on the theology of human beings (theological anthropology) before reading the second and third sections of the chapter (pp. 83–95). Answer each question true (T) or false (F). Tabulate the results for the whole class, discuss their significance, then read the sections, and focus on differences between where the class stands and what this book says.

   a. Human beings are a fragile mixture of nature and freedom, finitude and infinitude.

   b. We are primarily first individual selves, then enter into relationship with other selves and with the natural and social worlds.

   c. Freedom is an illusion, for all aspects of human behavior are determined by natural causes.

   d. Human beings are not limited by physical environments or satisfied by physical desires, but remain open to what is beyond, the infinite, the eternal horizon.

   e. Because tragic conflicts are endemic to the project of creating free beings distinct from God, God is the source of tragedy and suffering in the world.

   f. The transition from fallibility to fault (from the possibility to the actuality of sin) cannot be understood rationally but requires telling a story such as the "fall" of Adam and Eve.

   g. Saint Augustine was unduly pessimistic when he remarked that by sinning we lose the capacity not to sin.

   h. Sin is a defiance of divine prohibitions and commandments, for which human beings deserve to be punished.

   i. Flight (fear, sloth, failure, despair) is an even more pervasive and destructive form of sin than idolatry (rebellion against God, false attachment to finite goods).

   j. Sin issues in evil, and evil in turn magnifies and reinforces sin.

6. Read Genesis 3 aloud in class, following the procedures in exercise 4.

7. Feminist theologians have been critical of the story of the fall and the traditional doctrine of sin. What are the chief points they raise, and where do you stand in reference to their criticism? See the works by Wendy Farley, Kathleen Sands, and Marjorie Suchocki listed in the bibliography for chapter 4.

8. Is it proper to say that death is a form of evil, as this chapter claims on p. 95? How can this be if death is the natural fate that awaits all finite living beings? Analyze the argument, and determine where you stand. How should one comport oneself vis-à-vis death? Is death something to be feared, embraced, tolerated, avoided, defied, accepted?

9. The quest for justice was identified in chapter 1 as one of the distinctive challenges of the age in which we live. Does chapter 4 provide an adequate account of what makes for "justice" in human affairs and of how "injustice" has become such a pervasive and terrible form of evil? Is it fair to suggest that all of sin and evil point toward and result in conditions of injustice? Is injustice best understood by looking in detail at concrete situations or by developing a theory of sin and its corrupting effects on human nature? Think of the perspective of African American, feminist, gay and lesbian, or liberation theologians on this question.

10. Is the human condition a tragic one?

5

Jesus and Redemption:
Who and Where Is
Christ for Us Today?

The Problem of Interpreting Jesus

According to Christian faith, a saving incarnation of God's love has occurred and is definitively, not exclusively, associated with a specific human being. Thus the focus shifts and narrows as we turn our attention from cosmic patterns, natural processes, and anthropological structures to the concrete events of history, from the most universal to the most particular manifestations of God's love for the world—the same love, no matter how different the forms in which it appears. We rightly affirm the universality of God's love, which is available under any and all cultural and ethnic conditions, but we also have access to the universal only through the concrete and particular. The way in which particularity appears differs from religion to religion. For Christianity, the focus is on a specific historical figure who embodied a relationship to God that was absolute and unqualified, a matter of direct trust, without resentment, calculation, preoccupation with status, or cultic and moral paraphernalia. Thus this particular figure revealed the simplicity and universality of God's love; in him the redemptive power of love became palpably manifest.

Who and what was this figure, and how do we know him today? Access to a historical figure requires an interpretative framework. This framework becomes more decisive the more significant the figure is for our own lives. The problems involved in treating a typical sixteenth-century German pastor or a twentieth-century American preacher may be relatively simple, but they become complex when we are concerned with Martin Luther or Martin Luther King Jr. The interpretation of such figures is never completed; just because they are so important for us, each fresh angle of vision affords new insight. The events surrounding their lives and persons seem to remain contemporary. Here the interaction between past and present history is intensive because our own futures remain open and these past figures help to shape our own futures.

When we turn to the figure of Jesus of Nazareth, the situation reaches maximum complexity. For most Christians, he is not merely a significant figure of the historical past but a "saving event"—indeed, *the* saving event, which happened not just there and then but also happens here and now. This is what is meant by calling him "the Christ," the Anointed One, the Messiah of Israel. The "here and now" of Christ as saving event is at the heart of what Christians believe about Jesus as risen from the dead. We entrust our salvation or redemption not simply to a past memory but to a present, contemporary reality. Thus in *Christology*, we start with a present experience of this figure as alive and at work in the world, which not only provides the framework for interpreting the historical testimonies about Jesus found in the New Testament but also appears to shatter all historical possibilities. Perhaps, however, the presence of the risen Christ represents the most intensive actualization conceivable of the way in which a past historical figure can continue to live and have significance in the present, in which case the possibilities of history are not shattered but fulfilled in him. I return to this matter later. The point now is that the question of frameworks or models for interpretation becomes crucial because of the peculiarly intensive way that Christian communities have experienced Jesus as redemptively present, as involved in our own salvation.

Today the traditional models for interpreting Jesus as the Christ have come under severe attack, because the traditional models are perceived as ethnocentric, patriarchal, misogynist, anti-Judaic, exclusivist, and triumphalist. There is a good deal of truth to these criticisms. They point to the fact that Christian claims about Christ have always had a tendency to become overinflated and idolatrous, perhaps just because of the tremendous vitality created by the experience of the risen Christ, the experience of being filled by the Spirit of Christ. Spirit-filled persons can change the world, but they can also become fanatics. An extreme solution is to excise Christology from theology entirely, but what is left is no longer a distinctively Christian theology. A more viable option, and one that has been followed again and again by reform movements, is to turn back to the historical figure of Jesus as a corrective against the distorting ideologies by which he has been interpreted.

The difficulty is that we have no direct access to, and can never actually arrive at, the historical figure of Jesus. What we have, rather, is layer on layer of interpretation, which can be stripped away, but with a possibility of never finding a usable kernel. Scholars may be able to establish an outline of the career of Jesus, which can lay reasonable claim to historical validity, although it always retains the character of a construct based on secondary evidence, evidence that already interprets what it is witnessing to. The elements of this career include Jesus' baptism by John, his independent proclamation of the inbreaking kingdom of God, his attraction of a following, his parables and acts of healing, his table fellowship with marginalized folk, his conflict with religious and political authorities, his journey to Jerusalem to celebrate the Passover, and his provocation, arrest, trial, condemnation, and crucifixion.

Unavoidably, we must supplement this very limited historical-critical construction of the figure of Jesus by a theological or christological construction, which introduces interpretative models in an effort to elicit the coherence and meaning of the figure of Jesus Christ for human existence today, and it does so in a more explicit, holistic fashion than does a strictly historical sketch of what we can know about the public activity of Jesus. The theological construction relies not only on what we can learn from historical study but also on the experience of the Christian faith community in its ongoing encounter with the figure of the Christ, and it seeks to be faithful to the intention of early Christian kerygma in proclaiming Jesus to be the Messiah of God. Theology is a kind of fiction, an imaginative reconfiguration of what we know to be real. It is constrained by historical reality but not limited to it because it seeks to elicit the possibilities for creative transformation hidden in events and figures of the past.

Creative christological reconstructions are being set forth today by those who have raised questions about the adequacy of traditional views of Jesus for answering the most pressing and inescapable questions of our time. In Rosemary Radford Ruether's words, "These are the questions of political commitment in the light of poverty and oppression, the question of anti-Judaism and religious intolerance, the question of justice for the female half of the human race, and the question of human survival in the face of chronic environmental abuse." Written nearly twenty years ago, these words were prophetic. Much excellent work has been accomplished in the areas of feminist, womanist, African American, African, Asian, and Latin American Christologies. We are also beginning to think through the implications of Christology for the environmental crisis and for religious pluralism. These are the principal challenges we face at the beginning of the new millennium.

In this chapter, I focus on the question of religious pluralism, including whether Christians can affirm the identity of Jesus as the Christ without negating the people of Israel and their ongoing covenant with God. Dietrich Bonhoeffer's famous question, "What is Christ for us today?" has two aspects: Who is Christ and where is he to be found? The question is one not merely of identity but also of location. Is Christ in one place, here and there, everywhere, or nowhere? Are there incarnations of God's redemptive presence in other religions that are analogous to but genuinely different from Christ and that are also valid? To approach these questions, I believe a new way of interpreting the classical christological metaphor of *incarnation* must be found.

Jesus as the Incarnation of God's Wisdom

Chalcedonian Doctrine

A plurality of christological models appeared in the New Testament and in early theological writings, reminding us that the Christian movement was never monolithic. The incarnationist model came to prevail, but it was preceded by *adoptionism* and *kenoticism*, which claimed in various ways that Jesus, a righteous and holy man, was adopted as God's messianic "son" by the indwelling of a divine power that emptied itself (*kenosis*) of divinity and took on human form; and it was followed by *docetism*, which undercut the reality of Christ's human nature, asserting instead that he was a god in human disguise, who only appeared (*dokein*) to be human. In their extreme forms, adoptionism and docetism failed to bring divinity and humanity together in Jesus of Nazareth in a meaningful way.

The Council of *Chalcedon* addressed this dilemma in 451 C.E., but the solution that it proposed introduced marked tensions of a *metaphysical* as well as a religious kind. It affirmed two complete natures in Christ: a divine nature coessential with the Father and a human nature coessential with us. These two natures came together in a single person or hypostasis, which was that of the pre-existent Son of God or divine Logos. Even though the human nature was technically complete as to soul and body, it derived or borrowed its hypostasis, its personifying and individuating principle, from the divine nature. In other words, the personal self that appeared in Jesus of Nazareth was divine, not human. Jesus, while retaining a full human nature, in some literal sense simply *was* God. An ontological identity was posited between the personhood of Jesus and the Second Person of the Godhead. This was the so-called Logos-flesh or incarnationist Christology, which originated with the *Alexandrine theologians* and became the backbone of Catholic and Protestant orthodoxy.

Although the Chalcedonian doctrine attempted to articulate a profound, difficult-to-grasp truth about the co-presence of divinity and humanity in Christ, the difficulties with its way of thinking are all too evident today.

1. Incarnationist Christology diminished the humanity of Jesus, robbing him of personal agency as a historical figure. The logical extreme of this position was docetism: Jesus Christ was a god disguised in human flesh.

2. This Christology personified or hypostatized the Logos, regarding him as a gendered divine agent. To be sure, the ancient term *persona* originally referred to a functioning entity or mode of being rather than to a person, and "word" or "logos" is properly understood not as personal agency but as the power or action that constitutes personhood. Once *persona* terminology was introduced, however, personification became inevitable, along patriarchal lines.

3. This Christology reified Jesus' maleness (his contingent human particularity) into an ontological quality of Christ and God. Because the Second Person of the Godhead happens to be a male person (the

Logos or Son), only male flesh could become the bearer of the incarnate Lord; obviously it would be absurd to have a male person in a female body. From this derives the notion that only male priests can represent God. The argument works the other way as well in a vicious circularity: because the Word of God incarnate was a male, so also must be the Word of God eternal and therefore God himself.

4. Incarnationist Christology thought in terms not of relations or actions but of a duality of divine and human natures, hierarchically distinguished from each other, connected in terms of up-down movements from one plane of reality to another and merging into a strange composite, the "God-man." Nothing was more characteristic of the classical mythological worldview, and this difficulty adhered as well to classical adoptionism and kenoticism.

5. *Incarnationism* presupposed what today we seek to understand, namely, the divinity of Jesus. For modern persons, it is by no means self-evident, as it may have been for ancients, to start with the triune being of God and to ask how the Second Person of the Trinity assumed a human nature. We can speak about God, if at all, only by turning first to history and the historical figure of Jesus, but this figure was obscured and passed over by the metaphysics of orthodox Christology, which was unable to acknowledge the ways in which he too was limited and conditioned by historical context.

6. Classical Christology limited God's incarnate presence in the world to a single, "once and for all" event, which was rendered ontologically distinct from all other events in which God may be present. This *hapax* lends itself to Christian absolutism.

The Christ Gestalt: An Incarnate Praxis

To begin to respond to these difficulties, three moves seem necessary.

1. The connection between "Jesus" and "Christ" must be loosened or opened up. Following a suggestion of Raimundo Panikkar, let us affirm that "Jesus is the Christ" but not that "the Christ is (simply) Jesus." What we mean by "Christ" is shaped in a definitive way for Christians by the historical figure of Jesus of Nazareth, but what we mean by it is not limited to this figure and in fact is enriched and extended by encompassing more than one figure.

2. We must avoid the supernaturalism, patriarchalism, and docetism

of the Logos-flesh Christology, move beyond the impasse of the two natures doctrine entirely, and preserve the full humanity of Jesus while affirming God's incarnate presence in him.

3. We must explain how this incarnation is redemptive, that is, how it confronts and provides resources for dealing with the profound problem of human sin and its destructive consequences. The classical doctrine of *substitutionary atonement*, based on the juridical metaphor (guilt, penalty, satisfaction), and the assumption that it is primarily God who is injured by sin, are as little credible today as is the classical doctrine of incarnation.

These moves can best be accomplished in my view by thinking of God as redemptively present in the world, not as an individual human being (a "divine man") performing miraculous deeds (the traditional christological picture), or as a distinctive God-consciousness (Protestant liberal theology), or as a uniform inspiration, lure, or ideal such as that of "creative transformation" (some forms of process theology), but rather as creating *shapes* or *patterns of praxis* that have a transformative power in historical process, moving the process in specific, identifiable directions. To *shape* means to create a pattern in something, to inscribe or "incarnate" such a pattern in a physical body (literally) or in an ethical way of being in the world (metaphorically). The result of such a shaping activity can be named a "gestalt," using the German loan word for a pattern or integrated structure. The gestalts that have a transformative power in historical process are not abstract ideals but concrete, embodied practices with physical as well as ethical and spiritual consequences.

A shape or gestalt is not as impersonal as a universal influence or an abstract ideal because it connotes something dynamic, specific, structuring, but it avoids potentially misleading personifications of God's action. What God does in history is not to intervene in the sequence of causes and effects by way of special acts or to become a god disguised in human flesh or to speak literally through human speech, but to *shape* a multifaceted tranformative praxis. God does this by *giving, disclosing, engendering*, in some sense *being*, the normative shape, the paradigm of such a praxis. This divinely given gestalt, in which God is really present, shapes the historical gestalts by which structures of freedom, compassion, solidarity, and wholeness are built up. This gestalt is not a person or personal agent but a transpersonal

structure of praxis that grounds personal existence and builds interpersonal relationships because it is itself intrinsically relational, social,
communicative, pedagogical in character. I call it the "Christ-
gestalt," by which I mean what is for Christians the definitive shape
of God in history.

This gestalt became incarnate in the person of Jesus, in the bodily
as well as the ethical and spiritual dimensions of his being. *Crucifixion*
was something done to Jesus' body, and the most radical Christian
claim is that it was *God* who died on the cross, God who took the negation, suffering, and death of the human condition into God's very
being. God was in Jesus as the Christ precisely in his *not*-Godness, his
naturalness, his suffering and death, his contingency and limitation.
His physical body was significant not because it resembled divinity like
a Greek statue but in its very *un*godliness, its finitude and mortality, its
sexual and ethnic specificity. It is not as though a divine nature entered
into hypostatic union with human nature, appearing as a divine man.
It is rather that the all-too-human, crucified nature of Jesus became a
shape wherein God was definitively present in the world—the world
that in its very not-Godness, its otherness from God, is affirmed as a
moment within the life of God, remaining other even as it is encompassed by God. Suffering and tragedy are taken into divinity itself.

The Christ-gestalt formed in and around the person of Jesus of
Nazareth as a consequence of his distinctive mission, proclamation,
and death. His person in some sense became identical with the gestalt,
and by means of it after death he took on a new, communal identity.
The Christ-gestalt empowers the authentic being of human being,
which is a way of being in the world as a communion of free and compassionate persons before God; hence the more radically Jesus was
the Christ the more radically he was human. In this sense, he was truly
human as well as truly divine; these were not two natures in him but
simply his identity as a bearer of the Christ-gestalt. His person played
and continues to play a decisive role in mediating the shape of God
in history, which is the shape of love in freedom. Jesus' personal identity merged into this shape insofar as he simply *was* what he proclaimed and practiced. But Jesus' identity did not exhaust this shape,
which is a communal, not an individual shape. The Christ-gestalt
arose from the Judaic gestalt and developed into the ecclesial gestalt,
but it received its distinctive shape from Jesus' personal ministry (his

proclamation by word and deed of the coming of God's kingdom) and his personal death (his anguished sharing in the human condition and its tragedy). The way in which the Christ-gestalt is related to yet distinct from the gestalts of Judaism and other religions is considered in the final section of this chapter.

Jesus of Nazareth:
Shaped by the Wisdom of God

If we wish to ask how God was active in all of this, my answer is that the Christ-gestalt was engendered in Jesus of Nazareth by the *Wisdom of God*, which is a mode of God's spiritual presence in the world. God shapes spiritually, ethically, and corporeally by indwelling, moving, empowering, instructing, inspiring, and suffering with persons, communities, and other forms of life. These claims point in the direction of a Wisdom Christology and anticipate a theology of the Spirit.

In Phil. 2:5–11, Paul adopts an older christological hymn, which says that the "shape of God" (*morphē theou*) "emptied itself" and "took on" the "shape of a human being" (*schēmati . . . hōs anthrōpos*). This human shape, which was that of a servant (*morphē doulou*), entailed humility and obedience to the point of death but also exaltation and honor. In the original version of this hymn, the one who was in the shape of God and took on human shape most likely was understood to be the Wisdom of God (*sophia tou theou*). Using this text as a clue, I explore the idea that the Christ-gestalt formed in Jesus of Nazareth through the distinctive presence in him of the Wisdom of God.

For biblical Judaism, Wisdom is one of three primary mediators, hypostases, or personifications of divine power and presence; the other two are Spirit and Word. The three names point to the same basic reality, but they have distinctive aspects and emphases. Wisdom (*Sophia*) is consistently female in gender in Hebrew, Greek, and Latin, whereas Word (*Logos*) is consistently masculine, and Spirit (*Pneuma*) is mixed in gender. Wisdom is the most developed and widespread of these representations of God's presence and activity in the Hebrew Bible, and it is not inappropriate to conclude (as Elizabeth Johnson does) that "Sophia is Israel's God in female imagery," an imagery that places the stress on God's nearness, activity, compassion, communication, and pedagogy.

Only fragments of a Wisdom Christology remain in the canonical writings of the New Testament. From these fragments, we can form the picture that Wisdom or Sophia has many children, among whom are numbered the prophets and apostles, and that Sophia's children are likely to suffer abuse and rejection at the hands of this world. Her children are presently scattered about, but she will gather them and be vindicated by them; she will outlast the powerful, and her children will continue the struggle on behalf of God's project or kingdom (*basileia*).

Jesus of Nazareth is preeminent among these children because he proclaims the inbreaking of God's project and engages in a praxis of inclusive wholeness, gathering all who would follow. Sophia dwells in him fully but also transcends him, drawing him into contact with others, to whom he ministers and from whom he draws strength—women, tax collectors and sinners, Samaritans and Syro-Phoenicians, the sick and poor, children and the elderly, ultimately the whole of humanity. Jesus' followers will carry on Sophia's mission and message despite—indeed because of—his death, which is not a death of penal victimization but of heartbreaking empowerment. His message or project is the important thing, and Wisdom lives on in the continuing project. Jesus is the Christ—the shape of God in human shape—because he is the power of God and the Wisdom of God, although in the eyes of the world his power appears to be weakness and his wisdom foolishness (1 Cor. 1:18–25).

The Wisdom of God is not to be thought of literally as a divine person, agent, or hypostasis any more than the Word of God and the Spirit of God are to be thought of in such mythological terms. The Wisdom of God is rather the logical and pedagogical substance from which God's kingdom is built, and it is the spiritual power that shapes Jesus into becoming the proclaimer and bearer of the kingdom. The substance and power of divine Wisdom are what might be called "communicative love-in-freedom." Wisdom is a knowledge or insight that issues immediately into practice. Understood in this way, Wisdom encompasses both Logos and Spirit: it has a logos quality and a spiritual quality. Jesus is the Word of God and the Spirit of God because he is the Wisdom of God, the incarnation of God's caring, truthful, communicative Sophia, which sets us free from the lying, foolishness, and boasting of this world.

How does the Wisdom of God enter into and create the Christ-gestalt in Jesus of Nazareth? No theology can answer this question in the sense of providing a theoretical explanation. We must assume that God can appear and act in history, can enter into historical forms and figures, but how God does this remains a mystery. It seems clear to me that God does not act in history in the mode of material causality or of direct possession. The former has collapsed with the discrediting of the logic of divine sovereignty, and the latter is unattractive because it suggests that human consciousness is replaced by the possessing spirit, whether divine or demonic.

The Sophia-presence of God *is* a spiritual presence, but the question is how best to understand this. Anticipating what is said in the next chapter, I believe that Spirit indwells, empowers, instructs human spirit but does not displace it. Sophia defines the kind of Spirit that God's Spirit is—not a possessing, displacing, controlling Spirit, but a persuading, inviting, educing, communicating Spirit, acting in profound interaction with human spirit, indeed with the cosmos. God's indwelling Spirit has the quality of wisdom rather than of raw force; God is spiritually present not simply in individual human persons but in the foundational paradigms by which human personal and social existence is shaped redemptively. God's Spirit "in-spirits" human spirit, which is a social and ethical matrix before it is an individual person. It is not on Jesus alone but on Jesus in interaction with all of Wisdom's children that the Spirit dwells.

Three powerful images associated with Jesus have become superimposed to form that complex shape, the shape of Christ, which serves as a paradigm of Christian life in the world. The three are *basileia, cross,* and *resurrection.* They are what give the Christ-gestalt determinacy and content. Among them occurs an interplay of love and freedom by which God's redemptive presence in the world takes shape. Incarnation reaches its culmination with the crucifixion of the one who proclaimed God's inbreaking kingdom. Basileia and cross together define the shape of redemptive or liberating love; resurrection launches this shape into the world as an emancipatory praxis. The latter is an essential part of the picture because God's Wisdom is oriented to practices and transformation rather than to theoretical knowledge (although the latter is an appropriate part of theology).

The Shape of Communal Freedom: *Basileia*

The basileia, kingdom, or project of God is the central theme of Jesus' proclamation, especially as it takes the form of *parables*. The basileia itself is a parable of freedom, a realm of freedom, a place or structure or world where freedom, communion, justice, and truth prevail as the defining relationships among human beings instead of bondage, alienation, injustice, and illusion. The power of God establishes this parabolic clearing of freedom, although God does not directly appear in the clearing itself. The parables deconstruct the whole picture of monarchical-patriarchal-hierarchical rule to such an extent that the word *kingdom* is no longer usable, and we are left without an adequate term for what is envisioned. As a sign of this, the Greek word *basileia* can be left untranslated, or with the North American civil rights movement and the Central American liberation theologies, we can speak of the basileia as "God's freedom project."

The world evoked by the parables is a strange world. All the established economies that govern human behavior and relationships of power are shaken to the core by Jesus' proclamation of the "coming" and "nearness" of the basileia. The logic of domination, violence, reward, and punishment that prevails in the everyday world is challenged and replaced by a new logic, the logic of *grace*, compassion, freedom. The contents that make up this new world are familiar, but relations, values, behavior, consequences have been set askew and intensified to the point of extravagance, paradox, hyperbole. Thus we learn of a banquet to which literally everyone from off the streets is invited; of a tiny seed that grows into a great tree; of a labor policy that pays workers equally regardless of the amount of work; of a father who seems to care more for a prodigal son than a loyal son; of a joy in heaven over one sinner who repents, which is out of all correspondence with arithmetic proportion. The *surrealistic* qualities of the parables make them the opposite of the utilitarianism that governs the everyday world.

The gestalt of freedom, as it takes shape in the parables of Jesus, points unmistakably in the direction of a new communal existence that is intrinsically open to the other, the stranger, those who are marginalized and oppressed, those who belong to an alien culture, people, or religion. All false provincialisms break down—those based on race, class, sex, sexual preference, ethnic or national identity, religious piety, worldly success: none of these is relevant as a condition of God's redemptive presence, which is utterly gratuitous, open to all. This gestalt, found only at the margins of the everyday world, has a surreal quality without definable limits or boundaries. As such, it can serve as a paradigm or pattern of transformative praxis again and again in human affairs under radically different cultural conditions. This is how it works salvifically. There is nothing magical about it. It simply provides resources by which, again and again, we can break the grip of the dominant paradigms, battle against the debilitating fear that results in the flight from life or the dizzying illusion that we are god-like. With such resources at our disposal, we can find a purpose to life and even participate in the open-ended, always fragmentary project of building a new world.

The Radical Freedom of Jesus

Jesus embodied in his own personal existence the communal freedom of the basileia. He himself was a parable for what he proclaimed. In this sense, he became identical with the Christ-gestalt, but he did not exhaust or contain it. We can speak of three spheres of the *radical freedom* of Jesus: openness, community, selfhood. These are the very spheres that constitute human being (see chapter 4), but in the case of Jesus they have been rearranged in priority and importance.

Jesus' *openness* to God cannot be grasped directly but is visible only in the communal and personal structures of his life. Only rarely in the first three Gospels is his special relationship to God made explicit in his own words. The New Testament and Christian tradition referred to this relationship as one of divine "sonship." Jesus spoke of himself not as the "Son of God" but, if at all, as the "son of humanity" (*huios tou anthrōpou*), which is a generic construction meaning something like "the representative human being." Thus what is involved in Jesus' sonship is his *true humanity* as it was completed in radical openness to God, a God whom he knew not as distant but as near, father- and motherlike. Openness to God is constitutive of true humanity; it does not add anything extra or supramundane or "divine" to humanity. As the radically free person, Jesus was simply the fulfillment of human potentiality; he was the representative of humanity and as such the "son of God" but not literally God.

The distinction between God and the son of God holds also for those passages in the Gospels in which the "son of humanity" seems to be identified with the messianic figure who is coming on the clouds of heaven—a glorified yet still human figure. Whether Jesus was referring to himself in these passages or whether such passages are even attributable to Jesus are questions of ongoing scholarly debate. It is more likely that Jesus spoke of the "son of humanity" in other passages where the emphasis is on the son's earthly mission and suffering, but whether a self-reference was intended is uncertain.

Jesus' gathering of a new and liberated human *community* was the concrete, interactive form that his openness to God assumed. He not only proclaimed the inbreaking basileia but realized it under the specific conditions of his time and place. He condemned social injustice, religious arrogance, and political exploitation. He challenged the authority of established religious leaders, pressing for a much more radical reading of their scriptures. He identified himself with the poor, the powerless, the marginalized, having a table fellowship with them. He included women among his following, and they had a special relationship with him. He healed the sick and injured, forgave the sinful, and liberated those possessed by demonic powers.

The Gospels call special attention to the "compassionate" character of Jesus' relationship to the people, and he himself used the word *compassion* to describe the Good Samaritan, the father of the prodigal son, and the king of the unforgiving servant. This word is a very strong one in Greek and goes beyond even "sympathy." It means that Jesus took the misery and suffering surrounding him literally into himself, his viscera, so that it was as much his misery as it was theirs who suffered it. His being became totally a being-for-and-with-others. He also *received* compassion, care, erotic power from his companions. Jesus not only ministered but was ministered unto, so that a reciprocal communion of those bound together in solidarity and love, a solidarity unto death, came into being. The focus of his ministry was not on humanity's guilt-ridden disobedience of God, which required a substitutionary atonement, but rather on humanity's wounding of itself, its self-imposed and self-destructive bondage, which required liberating power and redemptive healing.

The Gospels also make it clear that Jesus manifested a remarkable authority, which was an expression of his *selfhood* or unique identity, an identity founded in openness to God and evident in the intense and direct character of his relationships with others. This authority was not something Jesus himself spoke about; it showed itself rather in the quality of his speech and actions. His hearers, friends and foes, recognized it, but he did not claim it or suggest that it could be legitimated by some future event such as his resurrection or second coming (these embellishments are a product of later tradition). The authority that marked Jesus' personal identity pointed away from himself; it was not a self-referential quality. Just as the new community he proclaimed and enacted was nonprovincial and nonalienating, so also the personal agency he exemplified was nonautonomous and not self-oriented.

It is important to recognize that Jesus' selfhood did not simply dissipate into nonidentity or emptiness: he was a strong and centered person who powerfully affected those who knew him. He did not advocate martyrdom or self-immolation. He taught that those who seek to save their life will lose it, and those who lose their life will find it (compare Matt. 16:25). There must be a finding as well as a losing of self. The great insight of his message was that the finding comes by way of losing, and the losing takes the form of living on behalf of others. The losing of self on the way to finding self is the fundamental and most demanding condition of human well-being.

The Shape of Suffering Love: The Cross

In the case of Jesus, the losing of self led to his death on a cross, although he did not seek or desire this death. The cross is the second powerful image by which the Christ-gestalt attains definition through its association with the figure of Jesus. It is not that there was something unique about Jesus' death; history has witnessed millions of executions, tortures, starvations, many more horrible than the one Jesus suffered. It is rather that *this* death coupled with *this* life generated a uniquely powerful and revelatory shape of God's presence in history.

Jesus' death on the cross is the culminating moment in the act of love by which God posits a world that is other than God, for it signifies God's unity with perishability, God's struggle with the annihilating power of nothingness, taking that power into God, converting it into the possibility of the new. Suffering and tragedy are incorporated into the divine life. The significance of the cross for God is that God becomes a suffering God. God's love for the world necessarily entails suffering, for God's love shares infinitely in the brokenness and anguish of the human condition.

The significance of the cross for humanity is its indication that all our historical projects of liberation ultimately fail. Jesus' project of announcing the inbreaking kingdom of God failed; the transfigured world of the parables was interrupted and displaced by scenes of betrayal, false charges, political dealings, weakness and vacillation, an angry mob, and an ugly finale on Golgotha. Jesus died with a question on his lips, "My God, my God, why have you forsaken me?" (Matt. 27:46). He who had proclaimed the saving nearness of God's *basileia* and had often spoken of God in intimate terms as *Abba* ("father") apparently experienced the abandonment and remoteness of God at the moment of death. Was this not a falsification of the truth of his entire message, a negation of his very being?

The shape of the cross is a question mark or a cancellation sign, a large X, which must be written across the shape of the basileia, reminding us that its vision of inclusive wholeness, of a liberated communion of free persons, forever remains marginal in this world, unable to dislodge the economy of domination and violence but only to disturb it, to disclose it for what it is, to reduce its scope and hegemony, perhaps to modify it somewhat, and above all to empower people to maintain a compassionate solidarity for and with one another in their struggle to make things better—as Jesus himself did, who died for the sake of all those who had joined or would join his cause, and indeed for those who would not. It reminds us that God does not rescue us from history or provide miraculous victories. God suffers alongside us, and it helps to know that God is there as a faithful friend, providing companionship, sharing our struggle and fate. The shape of the cross *crosses*, is superimposed on, that of the basileia vision, lending it the realism, clarity, and toughness necessary for its endurance in history as a transformative factor. Freedom is infused with an empathic, suffering love.

Yet, because the annihilating power of nothingness has been taken into God's being and converted there into the possibility of the new, it is possible for human beings to go on after such defeats as the crucifixion of Jesus. From death, new life arises. That death is not simply an end but a beginning, that it has the possibility of opening up new possibilities that did not exist before—this is the profoundest meaning of the cross, which was not only the death of Jesus but the death of God by which God undergoes, incorporates, and transforms death. The meaning of the cross is the victory of life over death, the resurrection from the dead.

The Risen Christ and the Work of Redemption

The Meaning and Reality of "Resurrection"

From the fusion of the images of *basileia* and *cross* emerges a third primary christological symbol, that of the *resurrection* of Jesus from the dead. Through the death that puts death to death, the shape of love-in-freedom imaged by the basileia passes from the limited ministry of Jesus and the basileia community that coalesced around him into the broad stream of human history, becoming a productive factor therein. The cross is the mediating link between the radical freedom of Jesus and "the glorious liberty of the children of God" (Rom. 8:21, KJV). As resurrection, the fused, superimposed images of basileia and cross, of freedom and love, acquire the resilience and realism necessary to endure in the midst of human tragedy, as well as the power to generate a continually transformative vision of a liberated community of free subjects. The Christ-gestalt that came to speech in Jesus' proclamation and mission now "comes to stand" in the world as the productive paradigm of worldly praxis. Jesus, whose identity was first established by the gestalt that formed in and around his person, now assumes a new, communal identity as the risen Christ, the body of all those who share in and contribute to the transformation of the world wrought by suffering love. Resurrection takes place when basileia community forms under the conditions of the cross.

The words used in the New Testament to describe the experience that lies at the heart of Christian faith—the experience of the living presence of the Crucified One—mean something like "awakening," "arising," "standing up." These words are often taken in the literal sense to suggest that Jesus' body was resuscitated and that he awoke from death as from a deep sleep. More commonly, they function in the Bible in a metaphorical sense to describe how someone "arises to an action" or is "installed in a function"—for example, the reference in the Letter to the Hebrews to the installation of Jesus as "a priest forever" (7:15–17). Following this clue, I suggest that "resurrection" (*anastasis*) means metaphorically that Jesus "comes to stand (*stasis*) in the midst of (*ana*) the world" as the agent or representative of God, engaged in a work of redemption. Jesus' agency is not exercised in some remote, otherworldly place but here and now, in our midst, on this earth.

This metaphorical interpretation of resurrection predominates in the New Testament after the stories of the empty tomb and appearances are left behind—that is, when we turn to the Pauline and Johannine writings and to the Letter to the Hebrews. The focus of interest is not on the miracle of resuscitating a dead man but on the saving, life-giving, redemptively transformative work of the risen Christ. This is not to say that these authors do not assume that resurrection is an event that happened to Jesus of Nazareth. They do assume that, but they make no attempt to explain how it happened. It is a deep mystery and a primary experience of faith. The event insofar as it can be talked about has an effect on, becomes visible in, the community of faith, indeed is constitutive of this community. Resurrection happens to both Jesus and the community, or *between* Jesus and the community, or between the small community that coalesced around Jesus and the great community of believers through time and space.

Paul links the themes of salvation and resurrection in various ways. For him, the event of salvation includes two elements, justification and newness of life, both of which are associated with the resurrection of Jesus from the dead (compare Rom. 4:24–25, 6:4–9). Likewise, for the Gospel of John, the resurrection is linked with the gift of eternal life, which has already been actualized in Jesus' earthly ministry and is evidenced by his life-giving power (John 11:25–26). Such life entails being "born anew . . . of the Spirit" (3:3–8), which means that the raising of Jesus is an upraising of the Spirit. The English word *resurrection* and its Latin root convey the same idea, namely, "the surging forth (*surgere*) again (*re*) of life out of death." The new life in question is transformed, faithful, liberated life. It is life in which fear is overcome and idolatry rejected; life in which the alienation and oppression of our corporate existence is healed; life in which the broken faith at the heart of sin is reconstructed.

How can this be? How can the past figure of Jesus serve not only as a historical model but as the living agent of the redemptive transformations we and our forebears have experienced in our own times and places? To reiterate Nicodemus's blunt query: How can a person be born anew if he or she is old, dying, or dead (John 3:4)?

Perhaps we can best approach the question negatively. On one hand, the resurrection of Jesus is something more than a historical influence or memory or a psychological event in the minds of believers. This is a rationalistic reduction of the resurrection experience. On the other hand, it is something other than a miracle of bodily resuscitation and quasi-physical immediacy, such as is implied by spiritualist visions or a transubstantiation of the eucharistic elements. This is a supernaturalist distortion, against which the empty tomb stories protect in a negative way, discouraging speculation about what happened to Jesus' body. "He is not here," the women are told at the tomb. "He is going ahead of you to Galilee" (Mark 16:6–7). What is risen is not the corpse of a dead man but a gestalt, a sociohistorical dynamic that coalesced in and around a specific human being and with which this human being is still identified.

The resurrection experience seems to have something to do with the fact that Jesus is *recognized* to be personally, efficaciously *present* in certain words, actions, and communal structures that evoke a new way of being in the world, a way of faithfulness, liberation, and love. This is the positive significance of the appearance stories, especially as found in Luke 24. Jesus is recognized to be present in the breaking of bread, that is, in the act of communion, of sharing. Presence occurs when recognition is evoked. Jesus is recognized and thus present in a structure or gestalt of word and act with which his personal being has become paradigmatically identified. What is recognized is not a human body per se but a shape of praxis embodied in a specific person in an unforgettable way; and it must be re-embodied in concrete persons ever anew for its redemptive potential to be released into the world.

So the presence in question is a *spiritual-ethical* presence; Jesus is no longer sensibly, physically present. The story in Luke 24 depicts a physical immediacy of Jesus with the disciples on the road to Emmaus, but he is not *present* to them because they have not recognized him, and when they do recognize him it is not because they have seen his body but because they have shared in a structure of praxis with which he is identified. The Christ-gestalt becomes incarnate for them in this concrete action—and so it happens again and again. The recognition of Jesus in this gestalt is a spiritual recognition, not a sensible or physical recognition; in fact, once he is recognized he vanishes from their sight.

Spiritual recognition is brought about by the witness or testimony of the Holy Spirit. We now live "in the Spirit," but not any Spirit; it is the Spirit of Jesus Christ, and thus we also live "in Christ." Continued reference to Christ is important, for we sense that the words, actions, and structures of the redeemed community are not our own doing but the doing of the One who is present through the gift of the Spirit and who defines or shapes the Spirit just as the Spirit is the power by which Christ is present. Christ (that is, the gestalt that coalesced in and around the figure of Jesus and with which he is still identified) empowers our actions and lives on in them even though we are instrumental in this process as the immediate, embodied actors. We, individually and collectively, are the body of the risen Christ, whereas Christ is the true subject or agent of our words and actions insofar as they are redemptive. The fact that Jesus as the Christ continues to live on in the world in this agential fashion is the mystery of his resurrection from the dead.

A suggestive theological interpretation of this *mystery* is provided by Karl Rahner. Already during his or her own lifetime, the individual human being exists in an open relation to the world, so that the world as a whole functions as the body of the individual, in addition to or as an extension of the individual's own body, and as the context of the latter. Through death and resurrection from the dead, this world relatedness is intensified and deepened: the human self becomes pancosmic, not acosmic. The world as a whole becomes its body, although the relations to this body are qualitatively different from those to the individual empirical body. Perhaps this is a way of understanding what Paul means by a "spiritual body" as distinguished from the "physical body" (1 Cor. 15:35–50). Self-identity after death is preserved, not by individuated physical continuity, but by participation in a community or spiritual realm of being in which the self is not lost but taken up into a higher unity or structure; there the self finds an identity that is founded outside itself.

Rahner suggests that the human self, "by surrendering its limited bodily structure in death, becomes open towards the universe and, in some way, a co-determining factor of the universe precisely in the latter's character as the ground of the personal life of other spiritual corporeal beings." Such a world presence or spiritual presence is possible for every human being; indeed, Rahner's point is that all human beings are in some sense co-responsible for the world and add something unique to it, in death as in life. The dead continue to have an effect on the living; resurrection brings what is dead and gone into play once again.

Thus Jesus' resurrection from the dead seems to be a specific instance of a universal human promise and possibility, which is consistent with what Paul says in 1 Cor. 15:12 ff.: "Now if Christ is proclaimed as raised from the dead, how can some of you say there is no resurrection of the dead? If there is no resurrection of the dead, then Christ has not been raised." Jesus' resurrection presence is more radical, and in that sense unique, by virtue of the absolutely fundamental way he co-determines the world, which in turn is a consequence of the fact that the Christ-gestalt took shape in and through his historical words, actions, and fate in a decisive way. The risen Jesus becomes a co-determining factor in the present constitution of the world whenever and wherever the Christ-gestalt (the fused shape of communal freedom and suffering love) takes shape anew. The identity of Jesus of Nazareth is borne through history by this gestalt—in so intensive a way that Jesus himself is felt to be personally present and active in the work of redemption.

All this takes place solely through the power of God. God contains within the divine life both the individual self and the world in which the risen self is newly embodied. Thus in rising into the world, we also rise into God.

The Work of Redemption

Redemption is appropriately understood today not in the literal sense of the purchase or buying back of freedom by a ransom or sacrifice or as the paying of a debt owed to God because of sin, but rather as a liberation or emancipation from whatever holds persons in bondage: ignorance, superstitions, idolatries, ideologies, anxieties, oppressive structures, xenophobias. Redemption, suggests Edward Farley, means the various processes by which human beings are turned away from idolatrous, alienating, destructive attachments and moved in the direction of goods such as courage, freedom, justice, faith, hope, love. God comes forth as God in redemptive transformations. *God* means the power that brings about redemption, and thus a conviction of the reality of God emerges along with a grasp of the meaning of God. Only the infinite, eternal God toward whom human beings are oriented can provide a foundation for their being so as to free them from idolatrous attachments to finite and temporal objects. No finite object can do this, for orientation to such an object only reinforces the idolatry.

Farley specifies certain "ciphers" that emerge from ways that redemption is experienced in the realms of human agency, the interhuman, and the social. In the sphere of human agency, these are the ciphers of founding, empowerment, and courage. Thereby the corrupted human passions, by which we become attached to our own interests and desires, can be transformed into an authentic subjectivity, empathic freedom for others, and wonder in the face of the real. In the sphere of the interhuman, the key cipher is that of reconciling love: the only thing that can break alienation between persons is the power of repentance and forgiveness. In the sphere of the sociopolitical, it is the cipher of justice, which aims toward a social redemption beyond all competing interests and political agendas.

The redemptive coming forth of God as God, Farley argues, does not take place by way of a divine-human immediacy that bypasses language, institutions, history. Being-founded is not a supernatural intervention in a human psyche, but rather occurs in connection with something that alters language, calls forth new communities, resymbolizes tradition. As a facticity or "work," redemption takes place in and through the historical. The "through-which" of redemption is the historical mediation of new stories, altered symbolics, new intersubjectivities, changed historical memories, new communities and traditions.

For Christians, the "through-which" of redemption focuses on the figure of Jesus, who embodied the shape of redemption in his life and death and by the power of resurrection becomes the agent of God's redemptive work in history. How does Jesus do this? By what means is his redemptive agency exercised? The classic models of redemption in Western theology—ransom, substitution, satisfaction—are concerned with transactions between God, the Devil, and sinful human beings. They are not helpful if sin is understood not as a captivity to supernatural powers or a violation of divine commands, but as a set of illusory disruptions in personal, interpersonal, social, cosmic, and religious relationships.

The oldest model of redemption in Christian theology is the pedagogical model, which is closely related to an understanding of Jesus as the incarnation of God's Wisdom. In the Gospels of Matthew and John, Jesus is called "Rabbi" or "Teacher," a salutation that links him more closely with Judaism than does any other christological title. At the beginning of the second century, the *Didache* and the Apostolic Fathers emphasized that what Christ imparts to us is new knowledge, fresh life, fellowship with God. He has rescued us from the darkness of error; because of enlightenment received from him, Christians have abandoned idolatry. His sufferings and death do not purchase remission of sins but rather challenge us to repentance. The *Apologists*, principally Justin Martyr, stressed that the primary purpose of the incarnation was didactic: as God's Logos or Wisdom, Christ imparts saving knowledge, breaking the spell of the devils who lead humanity astray. Tertullian understood Christ to be the illuminator and instructor of humankind. Clement of Alexandria in particular developed the idea that Christ is the *pedagogue* or "instructor," whereas Origen emphasized that through Christ humans lose their deadness and irrationality, becoming "divinely possessed and rational." Christ is "the pattern of the perfect life," the exemplar of true virtue into whose likeness Christians are transformed. Gregory of Nyssa and Augustine developed similar ideas. Augustine's understanding of redemption, as summarized by J. N. D. Kelly, is especially suggestive: "Both in his person and in what he has done, Christ, our mediator, has demonstrated God's wisdom and love. The spectacle of such love should have the effect of inciting us to love him in return. . . . More particularly, it should bestir our hearts to adore the humility of God which, as revealed in the incarnation, breaks our pride." This is "the profound mystery by which the bond of sin is broken."

These words seem to get at the heart of the matter. Jesus' teaching does not offer a set of prescriptions, laws, or doctrines, but rather a demonstration of wisdom—a way of being, acting, feeling, and think-ing that reorients lives. This teaching has the power profoundly to draw people out of their daily preoccupations and petty provin-cialisms into an encounter with the eternal, with ultimate truth and value, with unconditional love, with a radical, transformative free-dom. There is nothing magical about this process; it is utterly realis-tic and down to earth. It offers not so much a content as a way of seeing, feeling, desiring, thinking. It provides resources by which human beings can break the grip of idolatry and pride, battle against illusion and fear, orient themselves to the needs of others, find pur-pose in life, and participate in the open-ended, never-finished, always-ambiguous project of building a better world.

This teaching is unbreakably linked with the teacher, the one who enacted in his own life, ministry, suffering, and death the truth of the teaching. Here the teaching and the teacher are one and the same: they blend into each other in such a way that we understand the meaning of the teaching through the example of the teacher, and we grasp the identity of the teacher through the redemptive power of his teaching. If what has been said about resurrection has valid-ity, then the work of the teacher continues along with the teaching itself. The teacher founds the teaching and makes it efficacious. The teaching forms a gestalt—a shape of being and living, a practice of freedom, a growth in wisdom, a vision of wholeness, a resistance to evil, a rightness with God, which are the necessary conditions of human flourishing.

Christology and Religious Pluralism

An understanding of Jesus as the incarnation of God's Wisdom, whose redemption works pedagogically to transform life, opens Christology—much more readily than do the dominant models of incarnation and atonement—to the reality of cultural and religious pluralism, the struggle for justice, and the concern for nature. This section focuses on the first of these issues. The other issues are brought into play in the final chapter.

Looking first at the diversity of cultural streams within Christian-ity itself, we note that christological constructions drawing on indige-nous African traditions have portrayed Christ as the "wise ancestor" who places his descendants in contact with the source of life, or as the teacher and master of initiation, the elder of the community who initiates people into the way of life. The figure of the teacher, sage, or guru is especially prominent in Asian religions. Both Christ and Buddha—Jesus of Nazareth and Siddhartha Gautama—may be viewed as teachers of enlightenment and mediators of liberation who focused on the ultimate concerns of human beings in concrete situations. They taught a saving, practical knowledge rather than abstract truths, and they exemplified their teachings by their actions. To understand Christ as guru clearly stands in the trajectory of interpretations that have viewed Jesus as a teacher or rabbi, one filled by the Wisdom of God.

M. Thomas Thangaraj, working in the context of South India, suggests that this understanding is a more promising approach than that of regarding Jesus as an avatar or physical incarnation of deity. Gurus exist only *in relation* to disciples; it is the recognition and affirmation of the latter that constitute a guru's guruship. The guru *functions* as God to the disciples; he makes God's presence real to them. Above all, the guru *teaches*, and the central symbol of Jesus' teaching, the *basileia tou theou*, provides a vision of God, of human community, and of the problem of the human condition—the three themes addressed by every guru, according to Thangaraj. In virtue of his death and resurrection, Jesus himself became the way, the truth, and the life of which he spoke: the teacher-guru became the crucified guru, thus fundamentally modifying the received picture of a guru. If Christian theology is to break out of its Western mode and open itself to Asian, African, Hispanic, and Latin American resources, then its categories must become fluid and experimental.

Regarding the relation of Christianity to other religions, can we make universal claims on behalf of the salvation wrought by and in Christ, while recognizing the validity of comparable claims made by other religions and accepting that no individual or religion is able to grasp the totality of what is? John B. Cobb Jr. answers this question in the affirmative. He believes that we live in a time when the world needs Christ as never before. Christ is indeed the Way of Truth and Life—in the sense not of providing fixed guidelines but of trusting the Spirit that leads into all truth, breaking open hearers and letting them be transformed. The deeper our faith in Christ, the more open we become to truth wherever and however it is revealed. Jesus is the way that is open to other ways. To be centered on Christ requires us to be centered on others, to be open to and in relationship with others. The proposals I have offered about incarnation and redemption lend themselves to such an interpretation.

Cobb's insights have been developed by Paul F. Knitter. Christians, he says, may affirm that Jesus is a true and effective savior but not the only savior. Our own experience is limited and cannot take account of the experiences and messages of other saviors or religious figures. God's revelation in Jesus is not, therefore, *full, definitive,* and *unsurpassable.* In Jesus, we meet God fully but have not grasped the fullness of God, for Jesus is not God. The Logos or Wisdom of God was not confined to Jesus of Nazareth but has been active in the world before and after him. Being made aware of the fullness of truth is also to become aware that we do not know what that fullness contains: it is an inexhaustible mystery. Thus God's revelation in Jesus is not definitive if this term means *exhaustive* or *total.* But *definitive* can also refer to something that provides a definition or guideline, and I have used the term of Christ in the latter sense.

With these qualifications, Christians may announce Jesus to all peoples as God's *universal, decisive,* and *indispensable* manifestation of saving truth and grace. Following Knitter's formulations, we can say that the manifestation is universal insofar as the good news that Jesus proclaims is for all human beings, not just for some. It is decisive in that it calls individuals to a radical change of perspective and conduct. It is indispensable in that other peoples and other religions need to know Jesus too, need to recognize and accept the truth he reveals. The truth of other religions can be enhanced, clarified, and perhaps corrected through an encounter with the gospel of Jesus Christ. The reverse is also true, for there are other universal, decisive, and indispensable manifestations of divine reality besides Jesus. Human experience is too diverse, multifaceted, and culturally conditioned to expect that God's revelation is contained in a single mediator. To be efficacious, God's Word, Wisdom, or Spirit must appear under determinate conditions appropriate to different times, places, and cultures. With the early Christian Apologists, let us affirm the superabundance of God's self-communication: multiple word-seeds (*logoi spermatikoi*) are cast on the field of history.

The universal appears only concretely, in particular forms, but it is really the universal that appears this way. This is what religions are all about: the eternal and universal in a moment of time and in the shape of the particular. Today diverse cultural trajectories are communicating and interacting as never before. In this changed circumstance, the task is no longer principally one of mission and conversion, but rather, as John Hick suggests, of encouraging a free flow of religious influences and information together with individual freedom of choice. Peaceful dialogue among peoples of different faiths may lead in time to a degree of mutual transformation and even convergence in which two or more traditions can see themselves as different responses to the same ultimate mystery—even though disagreements are likely to remain about important aspects of faith and practice.

If we ask where Christ is for us today, the answer is that he is present in the ferment and commerce of religions, ministering and being ministered unto, engendering the peaceful dialogue, and enriching the lives of countless individuals of diverse traditions and cultures. Christ is also present in all those places throughout the world where people struggle for justice and for the harmonious dwelling together of God's creatures. The "where" of Christ is not limited to Christian history and institutions, just as the "who" of Christ is not limited to the individual figure Jesus.

We should not expect or desire that a single global religion will emerge. The continuing diversity of cultures and religions is of great value: through something like a balance of powers, the diversity blocks any single claim of absolute truth or monolithic rule. Differences should be honored and embraced, for every human being is enriched by them. Finding unity and wholeness expressed *through difference*, seeing the one *in the many*, appreciating that truth emerges in a diversity of ways—this in itself is a deep religious experience. Jesus of Nazareth contributes something unique and distinctive to the inexhaustible wholeness. His uniqueness, I have argued, is a function of the way in which the shape of Christ is formed by three powerful images associated with his life and death: *basileia, cross,* and *resurrection*. In this fashion, communal freedom and suffering love are fused to create a powerful gestalt of redemptive transformation. Jesus as the Christ, the Wisdom-filled *prophet* of Nazareth, binds together in a distinctive way the elements of mysticism and justice, spirituality and prophecy, wisdom and compassion, which are present in the great religions of the world in one form or another.

The most anguished of inter-religious relations for Christianity is that with Judaism, from which it evolved and against which it turned with fraternal fury. Despite the deep connection between the two religions, each has a distinctive genius. Part of the genius of Judaism has been its ability to survive in cultural environments hostile to its faith. This has given it a strong sense of spiritual community, ethical mission, and the hidden presence of the unnameable God. By avoiding the triumphalism and absolutism of much Christian theology, it is not only less dangerous to other religions but also more realistic about history: the messianic age has not come, and redemption here and now is partial, ambiguous, unfinished, tragic. These are insights that Christians can learn from Jews even as they attempt to work out an interpretation of Jesus as the Christ that is not anti-Jewish and indeed draws on resources in Judaism itself. The approach taken in this chapter, with its focus on Jesus as the prophet and teacher of Wisdom, is one such attempt.

It would be presumptuous of Christians to suggest that Christ alone is secretly at work in all religions where *salvation* is taking place. Christ is a determinate form of redemptive transformation. There are other such forms, other savior figures, who are both similar to and dissimilar from Christ. Early Christians recognized that the economy of the Spirit is different from the economy of Christ. According to the Gospel of John, the Spirit comes only when the Son departs. In truth, however, the Spirit precedes, accompanies, and follows the Son, and the reach of the Spirit exceeds that of the Son. Christ lends determinacy and shape to the Spirit for Christians, but the Spirit appears in other shapes in other religions. As the final figure of the divine life, the one that emerges from interaction between God and the world and brings the world to completion in God, the Spirit also brings Christian theology into close connection with other religious traditions. Spirit assumes a diversity of shapes, for the world from which it arises and in relation to which it manifests God's redemptive presence is incredibly diverse. Thus the Spirit introduces plurality and difference into the divine life. Yet the Spirit is also a point of contact, for religions can often share at the level of spirituality and wisdom while remaining in disagreement at the level of belief and doctrine. Christians should be thankful that theirs is a religion not only of God and of Christ but also of the Spirit.

EXERCISES

1. Discuss some of the issues involved in the difference between "the Jesus of history" and "the Christ of faith." Why can faith in Jesus as the Christ never simply rely on historical information about him? Why is historical information about Jesus nonetheless necessary for Christian faith? Debate this issue in class by letting one group answer the first question and another group the second; then compare the answers, and try to come to some resolution.

2. Do you agree that Christian claims about Jesus as the Christ have tended to be ethnocentric, patriarchal, misogynist, anti-Judaic, exclusivist, and triumphalist? Give some specific examples and counterexamples. What gives *us* the right, from *our* perspective, to make such a sweeping criticism of Christian tradition? What are the potential ideological distortions in our own efforts to interpret Jesus today?

3. The text passes quickly over the plurality of christological models that are found in the New Testament and early theological writings, and it offers some strong criticisms of classical "incarnationism"—the "Logos-flesh" Christology that became the backbone of Catholic and Protestant orthodoxy (see pp. 106–108). Yet the picture is more complex than this summary allows, and the development of Christology up to the Council of Chalcedon is a fascinating segment of intellectual history. As an independent exercise, engage in your own study of some aspect of this material. The following books are recommended: for New Testament christological patterns, John Knox, *The Humanity and Divinity of Christ*, chaps. 1–3; for the development of Christology in the patristic period, J. N. D. Kelly, *Early Christian Doctrines*, chaps. 6, 11–12; for a recent interpretation of biblical and classical Christologies, Roger Haight, *Jesus: Symbol of God*, chaps. 6–10. (See the bibliography for chapter 5.) After your own study, ask yourself (a) whether you agree or disagree with the criticisms offered in the present book, and (b) what resources are available in the biblical

and classical traditions for contemporary christological recon-struction. (The study can be done as a group project, with various aspects assigned to different persons.)

4. What is meant by the "Christ-gestalt"? How does this way of understanding the meaning of "Christ" differ from traditional ways ("Christ" as God's Word, Wisdom, or Son), and from mod-ern alternatives ("Christ" as a God-consciousness or as an ideal or power such as "creative transformation" or "divine empathy")? What does it share with these other ways? What is the relation-ship of Jesus to the Christ-gestalt? Discuss these questions in small groups; then come together, and share conclusions or unre-solved issues. The question beneath all of these questions is sim-ply how we are to understand God's redemptive presence in Jesus of Nazareth.

5. "Sophia defines the kind of Spirit that God's Spirit is—not a pos-sessing, displacing, controlling Spirit, but a persuading, inviting, educing, communicating Spirit, acting in profound interaction with human spirit, indeed with the cosmos" (p. 113). Write for ten minutes on this statement, explaining, questioning, or qualifying it. In class, read aloud a few statements as a basis for discussion.

6. Which aspects of the life, ministry, and fate of Jesus exemplify most profoundly the "incarnation" of God—the shape of God in human shape? Here are some candidates: birth and childhood, baptism by John, temptations, proclamation of God's inbreaking kingdom, parables and other sayings, miracles, healings, table fel-lowship with sinners and outcasts, arrest and condemnation, cru-cifixion, empty tomb, resurrection appearances. Assign each of these elements to one person or a small group for analysis; then share results, and determine which emerge as the most important elements.

7. Is it appropriate to speak of the death of Jesus on the cross as "the death of God"? What does such language mean? Does God liter-ally die? If God is dead, how can God save us from death itself and the effects or anticipations of death in history? If God is above such a thing as death, how relevant is God to our actual lives?

8. Does the "resurrection" of Jesus from the dead entail (a) the com-ing back to life of his crucified body, (b) a psychological event in the minds of believers, (c) a powerful historical memory and influ-

ence, (d) a new and ongoing corporate embodiment of the Christ-gestalt? Divide into four groups, each of which considers the arguments favoring one of these interpretations. Then discuss the matter in a plenary session. Are there other options?

9. The interpretation offered in this text of the redemptive work of Christ differs markedly from that provided by classical theories of atonement (ransom, defeat of Satan, deification, satisfaction, substitution). What do the terms *redemption* and *atonement* signify? What are the issues at stake here? Outline the options on the blackboard or sheet of paper or in a chat group, and try to decide which of them not only are intellectually compelling but also have the power to change lives. For information about classical theories of atonement, refer to one of the theological dictionaries listed in the bibliography or the works by Kelly (chaps. 7, 14) and Haight (chap. 8) mentioned in exercise 3.

10. Is it enough to understand Jesus as a teacher filled by God's Wisdom, whose teaching (for which he was put to death) had a radically transformative impact on human lives throughout history? What more is needed, if anything, to understand Jesus as redeemer or savior? Do you believe that the pedagogical model of redemption offered in this book opens Christology more readily than do other models to the reality of cultural and religious pluralism, the struggle for justice, and the concern for nature? Should such realities serve as criteria for soteriological claims, or should the latter be grounded primarily in scripture and authoritative tradition? As a way of beginning to work through these difficult questions, try imagining a concrete situation of human suffering, sin, or evil in which Jesus Christ might make a difference, asking yourself, "What kind of difference?" Several brief scripts on "Jesus making a difference" can be read and discussed in class or posted electronically.

11. How do you answer the question posed in the last section of this chapter: "Can we make universal claims on behalf of the salvation wrought by and in Christ, while recognizing the validity of comparable claims made by other religions and accepting that no individual or religion is able to grasp the totality of what is?" (p. 127). Can—indeed, must—there be a *diversity* of universal, decisive, and indispensable manifestations of saving truth and grace? Discuss in small groups and then in the whole class.

12. What does John Cobb mean when he says that the more we deepen our faith in Christ, the more open we become to truth wherever and however it is revealed? What is it about Christ that explains this paradox?

13. Debate the proposal that the challenge at the beginning of the twenty-first century is no longer principally one of mission and conversion but of peaceful dialogue and free flow of influences and information among world religions.

14. What can Christians learn from Jews about how redemption takes place in the world and about how Jesus might be understood to be the redeemer? In answer to the same question, what can Christians learn from Hindus, Buddhists, Muslims? Assign several members of a class to investigate the practices of salvation in other religions and to report their findings.

15. Who and where is Christ for us today?

6

The Age of the Spirit:
An Impossible Dream?

The Age of the Spirit

The ancient longing for a new age, a third age, the Age of the Spirit, as the medieval monk Joachim of Fiore named it, has a new relevance at the beginning of the third millennium of the common era. Joachim thought that the hierarchy of the church would no longer be necessary and that infidels would unite with Christians. His prophecies were out of touch with the realities of the second millennium, but today we have a new sense of urgency. It seems doubtful that humans can survive for another millennium on earth without a fundamental reorientation. We consume too many natural resources and inflict too much damage on the environment. We have created instruments of mass destruction that fanatics, terrorists, and sometimes even nations are willing to use, and we have developed an alarming tolerance for violence and systematic forms of injustice.

We find ourselves confronted by a bewildering variety of spiritualities across the globe, but we tend either to draw back into our own religious ghettos or to lose all religious identity. We sense that the institutional churches are becoming increasingly irrelevant to the real issues of today, and we are searching for new forms of spiritual community. Some of us may still hope that infidels will unite with Christians, but others look toward new forms of inter-religious sharing and cooperation. Throughout the world, there is a great yearning for

135

justice, but little sense of how to achieve it and considerable despair for the future. A symptom of both the yearning and the despair is that a multiplicity of fragmented, sometimes bizarre or destructive spiritualities litters the cultural landscape. None has proved to have staying power. Yet perhaps there is a Holy Spirit quite different from the secular spirits of our own devising.

Despite the neglect or subordination of the Holy Spirit in traditional theologies, the Spirit is the final and most encompassing figure of the divine life. God *is* Spirit in a way that God is not simply Father or Son. The abstract oneness of God and the specific incarnation of God are not lost but preserved in a richer, more inclusive unity. A pneumatocentric way of understanding God is not binary and linear but triadic and spiraling, moving interactively through God and the world into Spirit. The world becomes a constitutive moment in the life of God through the creative-redemptive-consummating work of the Spirit, which runs through history from beginning to end. Every age has the potential of being an age of the Spirit, and the Spirit is always coming. Our task is to understand the distinctive way that the Spirit may be at work today.

The Coming of the Spirit

Metaphors of Spirit

The Holy Spirit is never simply here or there but always coming, approaching, pervading, infusing. This insight is expressed by the biblical and classical *metaphors* that represent Spirit as a fluid, pervasive, intangible energy whose fundamental quality is vitality and freedom and whose fundamental purpose is to create, shape, and enliven. Four natural elements have traditionally been associated with Spirit: air, fire, light, water. These are material images of an immaterial vitality. All four are brought into play in the Psalmist's praise of God:

> You are clothed with honor and majesty,
>   wrapped in light as with a garment.
> You stretch out the heavens like a tent,
>   you set the beams of your chambers on the waters,
> you make the clouds your chariot,
>   you ride on the wings of the wind,

you make the winds your messengers,
    fire and flame your ministers. (Ps. 104:1–4)

The image of wind, moving air, and breath or breathing lies linguistically at the root of the words for Spirit in Semitic and Indo-European languages: *ruach* (Hebrew), *pneuma* (Greek), *spirare* (Latin), *Geist* (German). God's wind swept over the face of the waters, and God breathed the breath of life into human beings (Gen. 1:2; 2:7). Fire is closely associated with air because it is produced by the rapid fusion of oxygen with other substances. God's Spirit is a nonconsuming fire (Exod. 3:2) that releases incredible energy as it fuses with the elements of creation. It makes human tongues incandescent with language (Acts 2:2–4). Light has the same intangibility as breath. God creates light by breathing (by speaking, Gen. 1:3), but God also *is* light—a light that illuminates creatures by its radiance and saves them by its steadfastness (Ps. 36:9; John 1:5). God is also described (in Ps. 36:9) as the fountain of life, that is, as a source or wellspring, a fountain of living water (Jer. 2:13). Water is what is poured out, and the pouring out of Spirit is one of the most powerful images in the Hebrew Bible and the New Testament, suggesting its fluidity and pervasiveness.

If we move back slightly from these metaphors, we can say that Spirit is an immaterial vitality that enlivens and shapes material nature: it is the *energeia* that infuses all that is. Perhaps *energy* is a better metaphor of Spirit than is *power*, which often connotes *rule*. Following Paul Tillich, I have spoken of God's creative being as the power of being, but I also suggested that in relation to the natural world this power manifests itself as a primal and all-pervasive energy. Energy is simply that mysterious power that is active and at work in things—and that power (which need not be understood as ruling power) is God as Spirit.

Human Spirit

Spirit is not only the primal energy, the power of being, which infuses and enlivens all beings. It is also the distinctive essence of human being. In humans, the life-giving power also gives, or is, wisdom, intelligibility, reason. That is why in the Hebraic tradition Spirit (*ruach*), Wisdom (*hochmah*), and Word (*dabar*) are so closely linked, a linkage contained also in the German *Geist*, which means "mind" as well as "spirit." Spirit is intrinsically wise, rational, linguistic power; wisdom, logos, language are spiritual in the sense of breathing knowledge and will into materiality.

When Spirit enlivens human nature, the result is *consciousness*, which is at once physiological and psychological. It arises from the incredible system of synapses that is the brain, yet produces language, freedom, communication, centered personhood, self-relatedness mediated through other-relatedness. Today we are inclined to say that the essence of consciousness or selfhood, and hence also of human being as Spirit, is relationality. As personal selves or conscious subjects, we are an infinitely complex network of relationships—to our own bodies, to the material world through our bodies, to our past experiences through memory, to other personal spiritual beings through acts of recognition and intentionality, to the sociocultural world in which we are nurtured, to the universal power of being and meaning. Spirit is no one thing in this network but the network itself, pure relationality.

Far from being dualistic, Spirit is a mediating term: it is the rational manifested in the material, intelligibility in consciousness, language in speech; it is the unity of freedom and nature, self and body, individual and society, Creator and creation. Spirit over-reaches all these dichotomizing distinctions and levels the hierarchy between them. It is the relationality that holds things together even as it keeps them distinct. It is a desire or *eros* that is at once intellectual and sensuous. It posits and presupposes a material world but is itself immaterial and intangible, the ideality of reason, which itself is nothing but relationality. Spirit is intellect, reason, or wisdom as embodied in the media of consciousness and nature.

Divine Spirit

God too is Spirit insofar as God is present to, active in, embodied by that which is other than God, namely the natural and human worlds. Thus in scripture *Spirit* refers to that modality of divine activity whereby God indwells, empowers, energizes the forces of nature, the people of Israel, the ecclesial community, and individual persons. The Spirit is the indwelling power of God, which brings the natural and human worlds to consummation by bringing estranged and fallen beings back into everlasting, liberating communion with the one God, whose true and proper name is now Spirit.

Although in some sense personal, God's Spirit is not gendered. The word *spirit* is grammatically feminine in Hebrew, neuter in Greek, and masculine in Latin—a circumstance noted by Saint Jerome, who concluded that God as Spirit transcends the categories of sexuality. Spirit gives us a way of speaking of God that is not patriarchal or gender specific, and it should become the model for all talk about God, who is personal yet neither male nor female, but whose prophets are both male and female: "I will pour out my Spirit on all flesh; your sons and your daughters shall prophesy" (Joel 2:28).

When God's Spirit pours out, it engenders love and freedom. The Apostle Paul links the Spirit with both love and freedom in such a way that these become virtually indistinguishable qualities. It is through the Holy Spirit that "God's love has been poured into our hearts" (Rom. 5:5), and "the fruit of the Spirit is love" (Gal. 5:22). At the same time, Paul tells us that "the Lord is the Spirit, and where the Spirit of the Lord is, there is freedom" (2 Cor. 3:17). This is Paul's way of saying that the presence of God is no longer to be sought on Mount Sinai but in the Spirit, and that this presence liberates us from the law and all else that veils God from us. This is "the freedom of the glory of the children of God," our being set free from subjection to futility, which Paul describes as "the first fruits of the Spirit" in Rom. 8:21–23. Johannine imagery can be mixed with Pauline to suggest that when the Spirit of God is poured out it engenders not only love but also (in Abraham Lincoln's felicitous phrase) a "new birth of freedom." The Spirit is the power by which one is "born anew" (John 3:3–7), and the life into which one is newly born is a manifestation of freedom. Life is linked to freedom through the category of truth (John 8:32; 14:6), which means that it involves a liberation from "falsehood"—the Johannine equivalent to the Pauline "futility" as a characterization of the world's bondage. This is God's work in the world as Spirit.

The Emergence of Spirit

The Holy Spirit is not something that exists in advance as a supernatural person of the Godhead. There are no such pre-existing persons in God but rather potentials for relationships that become actual when

God creates the world. God does have a primordial self-relatedness, an inner complexity of identity-difference-mediation, but this relatedness should not be thought of mythologically as subsistent persons. The Spirit is an *emergent* person, generated from the interaction between God and the world, in the process of which the world is liberated and God is perfected. The Spirit comes into being through the pouring out of God in the world. The ancient biblical metaphor of "pouring" (Joel 2:28; Acts 2:17) accords nicely with the idea of God as *be-coming* in relation to the world. The appropriate trinitarian formula is God-World-Spirit, or God as World-Spirit, or God-in-Christ-in-the-world-as-Spirit. The Spirit proceeds from the emerging love between God and the world, and the Spirit then becomes the power of reconciling freedom in this differentiated love. Spirit is generated precisely in the process of pouring; it does not pre-exist the pouring as a bit of pre-packaged power. Wind cannot be boxed up; it happens when it blows. The blowing and pouring began with creation and continue as long as there is a relationship between Creator and creation. Although the mediating "third," the Spirit is not simply last in relation to God and Christ but contemporary. The Spirit both precedes and follows Christ.

In what sense is the Spirit personal? My view is that the inner-trinitarian relationships take on the character of personal subjects only in relation to the world. Christ is an individual historical subject although involved in a network of relationships; the Spirit is a social subject, a community of persons. God as a whole is personal, the one true and perfect person and the power of personhood, "the personi-fying person," as Karl Barth expressed it. What God "personifies" is not only God's creatures but God's own self, and this divine self-personification takes place through the evolutionary process, the emergence of human beings, the appearance of Christ, and the sending of the Spirit. God is already and not yet personal: "already" in the sense that real relations subsist within the oneness of God, "not yet" in the sense that the wholeness of God is an emergent sociality of which the Spirit is the pre-eminent figure.

The Relations of Spirit

These "relations" are phases in the emergence of Spirit or elements of the world from which and into which God-as-Spirit pours. Spirit is nothing without relations; it is precisely relationality, the moving air that permeates and enlivens things, the open space across which the wind of Spirit blows. The open space is the condition of possibility of relations; without it, everything would collapse into sameness. By entering into relations, Spirit loses its vagueness, takes on specificity and shape: it is this to which the language of "person" points.

God's Spirit takes on the shape of *many* created spirits: not just the spirits of living persons but of ancestors and animals as well as the spirits of plants, trees, rivers, mountains, storms and earthquakes, stars and planets. Belief in such spirits as intermediaries of both divine and demonic power is widespread in the primal religions, and it is presupposed by the Bible. Sophisticated Westerners dismiss such belief as superstitious, but it reflects the conviction that God is universally present and works through instrumentalities that are appropriate to concrete situations. Rather than over-riding the natural powers, God acts through them in ways that are complex, mysterious, and hidden. Thus God honors the integrity of the natural world while exercising sovereignty in it. This sovereignty is not absolute because demonic and destructive forces are also at work in the world, and humans become involved in the struggle between good and evil.

Theologians have hesitated to think of the Holy Spirit as World Spirit—Hegel's *Weltgeist*. Just this thought is required if the Spirit really emerges from the interaction between God and the world—the whole world, not just the human part of it. *World Spirit* does not mean spirit world, a special world or realm of spirits, preternatural beings hidden in natural things. Rather it means that the *whole* world is animated by Spirit and that Spirit proceeds from the whole world as God's body. It means that Spirit manifests itself in nature, that Spirit slumbers in nature and nature cries out to Spirit.

Can this be thought nonmythologically? Joel Kovel suggests that the manifestation of Spirit in nature takes the form of *eros* or *desire*—the great binding force of the universe, the cosmic law that all beings are connected, the longing to annihilate what cannot be annihilated, namely finitude and difference, "the roiling of indwelling nature striving toward spirit." Eros makes itself known through bodily desire or sexuality, a longing for and sharing in the other as belonging to an original and yet separated unity; but it appears as well in other forms of desire, intellectual, ascetic, aesthetic, religious. Perhaps the natural spirits are all expressions of this cosmic eros or allurement in modes appropriate to specific forms of life. Diverse parts of the universe call and reach out to one another in a thousand different voices. They are the voices of Spirit coalescing, of spirits witnessing to Spirit; but in nature Spirit has not yet found a fully spiritual counterpart.

Such a counterpart appears with the evolution of human beings as free and self-conscious persons. Both God and humans are quintessentially spirit, but they are so in different ways, and they relate to one another differently. Paul Tillich described the difference as follows. Whereas the divine Spirit "dwells" and "works in" the human spirit, the human spirit "stands out" from itself in a state of ecstasy under the impact of the divine Spirit. "If the divine Spirit breaks into the human spirit, this does not mean that it rests there, but that it drives the human spirit out of itself. The 'in' of the divine Spirit is an 'out' for the human spirit." Both of these expressions—"dwelling in," "standing out"—are metaphorical; we have no other way of expressing the mystery of the relationship of divine and human life. The "dwelling in" of the divine Spirit has the character of an utterly gratuitous gift; we cannot compel or control it; it comes on us in an awesome fashion. The "standing out" or *ec-stasis* of the human spirit does not destroy or dispossess its structure as a centered self but turns it from self-centeredness to reality centeredness, to connection with an elemental vitality.

When the divine Spirit dwells in or pours out on human spirits, something happens, says José Comblin, that cannot be wholly explained in normal human terms. "This *is* a human strength, but a human strength that suddenly comes upon people unprepared for it." The Holy Spirit acts in the form of human activity and depends on us to actualize itself. When it does so, however, we have what Comblin describes as "experiences of an unexpected transformation. People feel themselves taken hold of by new strength that makes them do things they had never thought of doing. Individuals and communities that had been downhearted, lacking in dynamism, resigned to the endless struggle for survival, discover themselves to be protagonists of a history far greater than themselves."

Comblin is speaking of experiences of liberation that come on oppressed and powerless people in Latin America, but the experience of the Spirit is similar for all people. When we find available the resources and power to go on when we have reached the end of the rope, when we are filled with hope in the midst of despair, when we receive the courage to act in the face of fear and discouragement—then we know that the Spirit has been "poured out" on us and that we are "standing out" into God. This is life in the Spirit, and it is what spirituality is all about. It is the most fundamental of all religious experiences, the experience of a renewing and empowering power.

The Spirit and Christ

The nature of the relationship of the Spirit to a particular human being, Jesus Christ, has involved an ancient and ongoing debate in Christian theology. Basically, the relationship has been conceived as a reciprocal dependence. *Christ is dependent on the Spirit* in a twofold sense. First, according to the adoptionist and kenotic Christologies (which are more retrievable today than is strict incarnationism), what makes Jesus the Christ is the indwelling of the Holy Spirit. His spirit was shaped by the divine Spirit (Sophia/Spirit, according to the earliest traditions) in ways regarded as disclosive and normative by the Christian community. The Spirit engenders the Christ-gestalt in Jesus of Nazareth. Second, the shape of the risen Christ is no longer historical and sensible but present and spiritual. The Spirit is the instrument of Christ's contemporary presence to communities of believers, the means by which the Christ-gestalt fans and flames out to embrace the whole world. Christ is no longer incarnate in the individual body of Jesus of Nazareth but rather is infused into the world by the Spirit, which shapes corporate bodies of redemptive praxis.

The Spirit is dependent on Christ in one fundamental sense: the Spirit known by the Christian community of faith is not any spirit or a multiplicity of spirits but the Spirit defined, profiled, discerned by the concrete configuration of the Christ-gestalt in Jesus of Nazareth. Just how we understand this dependence makes a considerable difference. Fearful of any tendency to view the Spirit as superseding Christ and rendering him superfluous, much of Western theology, Protestant in particular, has emphasized that the function of the Spirit is essentially subservient and instrumental to the work of Christ. This view makes much of the fact that, according to the Gospel of John, the Spirit comes after Christ in the divine economy; it draws support from a

modification to the *Nicene Creed* adopted in 589 C.E., specifying that
the Holy Spirit proceeds "from the Father *and from the Son*"—a modification not accepted by the Eastern Church. The effect of this
filioque clause was to marginalize the spiritual movements in Western
Christendom and to encourage a narrow christocentrism.

We find ourselves walking a tightrope, guarding against the dan-
gers of both subordinationism (of the Spirit to Christ) and superses-
sionism (of Christ by the Spirit). The greater threat today for most
Western Christians remains the former. The challenge is to work out
a theology of the Spirit that embraces and empowers the Christ-
gestalt without either superseding it or being subordinated to it. A
renewed theology of the Spirit provides a way of responding to concerns raised by feminism, liberation movements, ecology, and religious pluralism. Yet we must be wary of facile talk about a new age,
the Age of the Spirit, a "third kingdom" consisting of a purely spiritual religion. Such a kingdom, cut off from historical reality and
determinate traditions, will never arrive, or, if its arrival is announced,
it will likely take a fanatic, destructive form such as the Nazi Third
Reich.

Nazism was in fact a fascist form of spirituality that held considerable appeal to those looking for a spiritual rejuvenation in the context
of the crisis afflicting Germany and late-bourgeois culture. It is striking that the most fanatic ideologies often have a spiritual quality, and
their leaders sometimes seem to be possessed. There are many spirits at loose in the world—false and evil spirits, demonic and destructive spirits. This fact is not attributable to an evil god, a real Satan or
Devil, or to an evil principle in the godhead. Rather spirit is a potency
whose specific character is determined by the elements with which it
reacts. It can readily be distorted by human sin, and sin becomes
objectified in structures that take on a demonic, spiritlike quality. Evil
mimics the good, the demonic mimics the divine, destructive spirits
mimic the Holy Spirit. Human beings strive to be "like God," and
they are remarkably successful at this deception.

Because of this mimicry, this pervasive deception, it is necessary
to be able to *discern* the spirits. For Christians, the shape of Christ
incarnate and risen is the basis for discerning a Spirit that is true and
holy, a Spirit of suffering love and reconciling freedom. It is naive,
however, to think that this Christ, to whom an authoritative scrip-

ture attests, provides an absolute criterion by which to judge history, for Christ is known and interpreted only through the witness of the Spirit in concrete situations. It is the complex interplay of Christ and Spirit that enables Christians to make always ambiguous and relative judgments in history. There is no absolute guarantee against succumbing to illusion and self-deception, no sacred authority to which to appeal, but rather a constant struggle of interpretation. The Spirit is our companion in that struggle, but how we respond to the Spirit is up to us. It behooves us to respond critically, suspicious of all claims to authority, rather than in a state of uncritical enthusiasm, whether for Christ or for nation. The critical principle is the true spiritual principle.

In arguing for the emergence of the Spirit from the interaction of God and the world, I have advocated a double procession. The Spirit proceeds not from the Father and the Son but from God and the world. Thus there can be no question of a subordination of the Spirit to Christ, but does not such a proposal face the reverse danger of an uncritical spiritualism? I offer two observations.

First, the world that is the figure of God in the element of difference is not just any world but (from a Christian perspective) the world in process of being shaped and configured by Christ. Hence the world from which the *Holy* Spirit proceeds is a *christomorphizing* world. The world does not outgrow Christ but grows into Christ, and it does so through the Spirit, which both precedes and follows the historical figure around whom the shape of Christ coalesced. The Spirit emerges neither independently of Christ nor in sole dependence on him. The relationship is one of a thoroughgoing reciprocity.

Second, the theological tradition thought only in terms of the opposition between Christ and Antichrist. There surely are Antichrists, and Hitler was one of them, but there are also those who are *other* than Christ, different from Christ, without being antagonistic toward Christ. Today we must recognize a plurality of saving shapes of divine presence, and we should be able to affirm that the Spirit proceeds from this plurality, not from Christ alone. Ethical judgments about what is truly *anti-* (antihuman, anticosmic, antichristic, antispiritual) are not thereby eviscerated but arise from a communicative consensus rather than from a single revelation.

A Spirituality for Today: Ecology, Justice, and Pluralism

The work of the Holy Spirit has traditionally been approached in terms of two sets of metaphors: the Spirit as *Paraclete*, Illuminator, and Comforter; and the Spirit as Sanctifier and Perfecter. The first points to the inward and subjective aspects of the Spirit's work as it builds up a redemptive community in the world. The second points to the Spirit's eschatological work as it brings all things to completion in God. These are ongoing works of the Spirit common to every age, but each age also offers distinctive challenges that help to define Christian spirituality for particular times and places. In the early church it was the struggle against cultural assimilation; in the Middle Ages, a profound sense of guilt and mortality; for the Reformers, the question of justification and forgiveness; for modern Protestantism, the impact of the *Enlightenment* and scientific knowledge; for twentieth-century Christians, the experience of meaninglessness and alienation. (This is a very oversimplified picture of a complex interweaving of factors in every age.)

At the beginning of the third millennium, three issues seem to pose the profoundest challenge to the future flourishing of human beings on the earth. I have identified them as *ecology, justice,* and *pluralism*; I believe they offer Christians the prospect of a spirituality—a way of being and living in and through the Spirit—that is neither sentimental, fanatic, nor despairing. These cultural issues have been discussed in relation to the theological themes of God and the world, human nature and evil, and Christ and redemption. They come together in the Spirit, whose work for our time can be defined in relation to them. Our age too has the prospect of being an age of the Spirit. It is not an impossible dream.

Ecology: Spirit and Cosmos

An ecological understanding of the world introduces a kind of spirituality. The deep insight of ecology is that the natural world is made up of a highly complex, delicate, yet resilient web of relations and dynamic systems. The operative metaphor is *organic*, not *mechanical*, and *organic* suggests a cosmic body that is alive, fluid, unpredictable, suffused by energy. *Energy* is a metaphor for a power that has many qualities of spirit. It is not identifiable with visible, substantial entities but is what radiates through them, gives them life and movement. It works in a mysterious rhythm of waves and particles, which is not precisely measurable and produces ever-new patterns from a chaotic flux. Post-Einsteinian scientific cosmologies are much closer to a religious apprehension of the cosmos than were the mechanical models that dominated from the late seventeenth to the early twentieth centuries. The new science generates a distinctive spirituality that is both consonant with yet different from religious experience.

We know that if we continue to use this wonderful planet as a resource to be consumed by humans in the pursuit of material extravagance, we will destroy it. We create the illusion of technological fixes that will tap into the limitless energy of the sun or enable humans to escape to other planets after they ruin this one, but there are no technological fixes to what is essentially a disease of the spirit. Our knowledge of the environment, however, remains largely theoretical, and politicians and scientists have as yet found no way to use this knowledge to establish policies that make a significant difference. Market interests keep shoving an ecological sensibility to the back burner of the political agenda. We tinker around the edges.

A revolution of the Spirit is called for. This is not something that the human spirit can achieve on its own, moved as it is by its proclivity toward self-centeredness and consumption. Something is needed to draw us out of ourselves into profound communion with the natural world, with the cosmos. This must be the work of God's Spirit as cosmic or World Spirit, calling to us out of the depths and heights, out of rocks and flowers, out of near and distant kin among animals. Such a Spirit requires us to affirm as good and precious what has been created, to consume as little as possible, and to recycle what we have used. It calls on us in our own activities to strive for beauty and goodness, to enhance life rather than destroy it, to share rather than accumulate resources, to work cooperatively rather than competitively (acknowledging that competition and resistance are sometimes unavoidable). Only the Holy Spirit can transform our instinct for personal survival into a commitment to cosmic survival. Christian communities of faith could be at the forefront of calling forth an ecological spirituality.

Justice: Spirit and History

Human history has been principally a history of injustice, violence, and suffering. This was foreshadowed by the primeval rebellion and fratricide recounted in Genesis; even before civilization began, a flood was required to purge the earth of evil. The great civilizations that we admire were built at an appalling human cost by persons who acted with ruthless determination. The philosopher Hegel, who was profoundly aware of the evil, passion, self-interest, and violence in human affairs, described history as "an altar on which the happiness of nations, the wisdom of states, and the virtue of individuals are slaughtered." With such an image in mind, he suggested, it is tempting to take refuge in fatalism, viewing history as ultimately absurd or futile, busying ourselves with private aims and interests, retreating "into that selfish complacency which, . . . from a secure position, smugly looks on at the distant spectacle of confusion and wreckage."

Something is needed to wrench us out of complacency, to awaken in us not only a yearning for justice but a determination to achieve justice, knowing that the task is never ending. If we do not awaken from our complacency, the enhanced instruments of violence made possible by modern technology (ranging from handguns to chemical and biological warfare) will make of history a slaughterhouse. The slaughter will not remain a distant spectacle but will engulf all of us, for the world is interconnected as never before. A Spirit must call to us out of the cries of the victims of history. It is the Spirit of the Crucified One, telling us that it is possible to find love in the midst of anguish, freedom in the midst of oppression, hope in the midst of despair. Divine strength and resources are available if we open ourselves to them.

A spiritual awakening is desperately needed, but this must be an awakening oriented not merely to individual but to social salvation—not merely to conversions of the heart but to the creation of more humane political and economic institutions. If the third millennium does not find a way to transform the history of injustice into a history of justice, the history of violence into a history of peace, it is likely to be the last of the human era. What is needed are not fantasy solutions but a utopian realism that relies on a balance of powers, cooperative efforts at restraining criminals and tyrants, the education of citizens to democracy, and social goals such as the elimination of poverty, prejudice, and gross inequities. Christian communities of faith could contribute to creating a public ethos in which justice and peace are achievable goals.

Pluralism: Spirit and Religions

The Spirit is moving through the great religious traditions. It has always been so, but today communication, travel, and research bring these traditions together as never before. We now have a far richer and more accurate sense of the diversity of religious manifestations from which the Spirit proceeds—for it proceeds from the interaction of God and the whole world. Can we Christians really affirm that the Spirit of Jesus Christ is also the Spirit of Abraham and Moses, Socrates and Plato, the Lamas and Buddhas, Krishna and Confucius, Muhammad and Bahā'Allāh, Gandhi and King? There is something frightening and disorienting about this diversity, a sense of something out of control. Indeed something is out of (our) control, namely, the Spirit itself, which blows where it will and pours itself into many figures.

Even God does not control the shapes that Spirit assumes, but we have reason to believe that God creates the world and sends the Spirit toward an end—an end that can never be fully grasped but includes such goals as an enhancement of life and diversity, a harmonious dwelling together of the whole cosmos, a struggle to heal tragic conflicts, a growth in love and justice, enlightenment and wisdom, goodness and beauty. The reason for believing this is that such goals and values are affirmed, often in strikingly different ways, by the great religions and cultures of the world. A few deep and enduring values have emerged from the refinery of history, despite the recalcitrance and self-centeredness of human beings, and we can take this fact as proof that God's Spirit has been at work in the great cultural trajectories. These values are often distorted by the interests that produced them, and in every culture outright contradictions and ambiguities occur. The special challenge today is to keep the refining process going by encouraging religions, through dialogue and interaction, to identify one anothers' blind spots and to contribute reciprocally to the spiritual growth of all. The outcome will be not a melding of religions but a deepened insight into each tradition and a sharing of resources.

The Holy Spirit provides a window for Christians onto the diversity and plurality of world religions. A theology of the Spirit is a Christian way of construing this diversity and plurality, relating it to the purposes, activity, and being of God. It is only one such construal, and it must accept that other religions interpret the diversity differently. It has no monopoly on the truth. If faith in the Spirit of Jesus Christ means openness to truth wherever it manifests itself, Christian communities of faith should be at the forefront of the dialogical process, offering their own deep insights and eager to learn from Jews and Muslims, Hindus and Buddhists, the primal and indigenous religions. Obviously not everything in a religious tradition is true or helpful, and critical judgments are unavoidable. Such judgments are possible in an open network of interpretation.

Beyond Accusation and Consolation: A Possible Dream

Christian communities of faith are held back from embracing a new spirituality because they are trapped in old forms of religiousness. The novelist George Eliot said that the supreme subject with which she found herself engaged is "how far the religion of the future must be one that enables us to do without consolation." To Harriet Beecher Stowe, she wrote that "a religion more perfect than any yet prevalent, must express less care for personal consolation, and a more deeply-awing sense of responsibility to man." By "personal consolation," she meant a preoccupation with the salvation of our own souls, a calculation of rewards and punishments, a desire to be rescued from present sufferings, a fear of vengeance combined with a willingness to have it inflicted on others, a holding onto our own way instead of reaching out to other ways. Such attitudes have a corrupting effect on true piety, and they drove George Eliot away from the evangelical Christianity she embraced as a young woman. "I cannot rank among my principles of action a fear of vengeance eternal, gratitude for predestined salvation, or a revelation of future glories as a reward."

In writing this, she anticipated what the philosopher Paul Ricoeur has described as "the rotten points" present in every religion—accusation and consolation, taboo and shelter, the fear of punishment and the desire for protection. "In destroying the shelter offered by religion and liberating men from the taboos imposed by religion," Ricoeur said, "atheism clears the ground for a faith beyond accusation and consolation."

A faith beyond accusation and consolation—this must be a gift of the Holy Spirit. Such a faith frees persons from dependence on a scheme of salvation controlled by the logic of reward and punishment, the logic of the everyday world as opposed to the logic of grace that suffuses God's kingdom. Atheism clears the ground for such a faith because it destroys the idolatrous deity we are all too ready to worship—a Supreme Being who manages the affairs of the world to our own best advantage. In truth, God suffers in history and does not rescue us from disasters or reverse the effects of wrongdoing. Yet we can believe that God's Spirit does provide strength and resources to go on, to start over, to make the best of the circumstances that present themselves. Redemptive transformations do occur in human lives, but they are always partial, fragmentary, ambiguous. We can strive for the achievement of some possible better while avoiding the illusion of perfection or the despair of inevitability.

Having such faith is a very possible dream, but it requires a community to sustain it—a community of friends who lend one another courage, comfort, and resolve to act under difficult circumstances. Yet human friends alone are not enough, given the fragility and transience of the human condition. George Eliot observed that we need a God who not only sympathizes with our suffering but will *pour new life* into our languid love and *strengthen* our vacillating resolve. "Pouring" and "strengthening" are metaphors associated with the Holy Spirit. God does not act directly, miraculously, superhumanly, but through the indwelling of the Spirit and the mediation of human friends. Jesus himself was such a friend, but he could not act alone. He needed a community of brothers and sisters, and he is present today through an ongoing community of friends and saints, which knows no boundaries of space and time, institution and creed. This is the community of the Spirit. Spirit in the trope of Wisdom, we are told, "passes into holy souls and makes them friends of God, and prophets" (Wisd. of Sol. 7:27).

There are two kinds of communities. One is an aggregate of individuals who exist mostly in isolation and from whom social unity must be coerced. The other is a communion of love in which individuality is not suppressed but elevated to a higher cause, that of freedom, truth, compassion, fellowship. Only the latter is a spiritual community. It is spiritual because it is grounded in acts of mutual forgiveness and understanding, which release the other to be other while remaining in relationship to the whole. God as Holy Spirit *is* the event of release, forgiveness, and understanding that makes community possible. A divine community-creating power is needed because of the egoism, blindness, and conflicts that pervade the human social world. A unity that does not destroy but embraces finite subjects, healing their mutual hostility, bringing good out of evil, is attributable only to a transcendent power, not to immanent human resources. We need an Interpreter—the Holy Spirit—who breaks through the blockages and isolation of human existence and interprets all to all. "Interpreter" is Josiah Royce's ingenious translation of the traditional name of the Holy Spirit, *Paraclete*—an advocate, intercessor, or intermediary. Such interpretation has not only a reconciling but also an emancipatory effect in the world because conditions of systematic distortion and exploitation block communication. Thus the spiritual community is not only a beloved community (as Royce, an early twentieth-century American philosopher, called it, and after him Howard Thurman and Martin Luther King Jr.) but also a liberated and free community, a redeemed community.

Living in the community of the Spirit, we find ourselves beyond accusation and consolation. Such a community is not coerced by taboos, regulations, or threats of punishment. It provides the nurturing context in which human beings can flourish. In it we have no need for a calculus of deeds and consequences oriented to the salvation of our souls. In truth, we humans lack information about the state of existence after death, and the less we are preoccupied with our personal destiny the better. We need only have faith that all of creation is preserved and glorified in the eternal life of God. The Spirit's work of sanctification is oriented to engendering a communion of friends, prophets, and saints within history. This communion runs through history and knows no spatial boundaries. The creation of a great fellowship among all the peoples of earth is the true end of history within history.

Yet history itself has an end, the consummation of all things in God. An affirmation of this transhistorical consummation is important because it provides a horizon for historical praxis. Does this consummation occur only at the end of time or in every moment of time? The theological tradition has usually understood it to be the former, by way of a chronologically future package of last things, the *eschaton*. The notion of an abrupt and catastrophic end, however, is a literalized and misleading myth (the cosmos is more likely to die a slow death), and it devalues the present. I think we must affirm that God is not only a chronologically future terminus of world history but an ever-present one, a terminus that is also a transition, a passing over into the eternal historicality of God. We experience this transition both in the fullest moments of our living and in the final moment of our dying. God is always there, always available. This dimension of depth, of spirituality, funds liberation and alters the horizon in which historical praxis is undertaken. In affirming this, we must not lose contact with temporal process and historical change. We are empowered to struggle for a better tomorrow *just because* we are sustained by God's amazing grace, suffused by divine presence, today. The transhistorical horizon invigorates the historical field. Far from providing a consolation for worldly travail, it forces us back into the travail with renewed energy. Confident that our eternal destiny is in God's hands, we do not fear death and are not enthralled by worldly powers.

Obviously we have no adequate way of describing a transhistorical *consummation* because all our categories presuppose worldly distinctions and relationships. Here theological language becomes highly paradoxical and poetic, as in the imagery of the eschatological banquet found in Jesus' parables. Paul Tillich has suggested that the consummation has three aspects: the elevation of the temporal into eternity, the exposure of the negative as negative, and the conquest of the ambiguities of life. God elevates the positive content of history into eternity and at the same time excludes the negative from participation in it, although the negative does not simply disappear: it remains in the eternal memory of God as that which has been overcome. Everything good that has been created in history is preserved, indeed amplified. The ambiguities of life—identified by Tillich as disintegration, destructiveness, profanization—are conquered by the divine centeredness or love, the divine creativity, and the divine freedom. All this is going on here and now, not just at some remote point in the future.

Alfred North Whitehead suggests that the creative process does not stop with the consummation of all things in God; rather the perfected actualities of the world pass back into the temporal-historical process as inspirations or lures for new occasions of experience. In this sense, the kingdom of God is with us today. The influence of God on the world and of the world on God is an ongoing spiral: God's initial creativity, the events of nature and history, the perfection of things in God, the love of God for the world.

As for the question that tends to preoccupy us, that of the destiny of individual persons, I have argued that the metaphor of resurrection does not mean the coming back to life of a dead person, and thus it cannot entail the continuation of a particular stream of consciousness. Rather it suggests the idea of taking up an action or function by which our identity is preserved in a new communal, corporate embodiment that is spiritual in character. Self-identity after death is preserved, not by individuated physical continuity, but by participation in a community or spiritual realm of being in which the self is not lost but is taken up into a higher unity of structure of which we have only a dim apprehension. The self finds an identity that is founded outside itself. In this way, our life surges forth again after the hiatus of death. The hiatus is marked by the two kinds of embodiment: the human self "is sown a physical body, it is raised a spiritual body" (1 Cor. 15:44). The spiritual body is a spiritual community, a nexus of relationships engendered by the Spirit.

The ultimate spiritual community into which we are raised is God's own communal being as the whole or all that encompasses all that is, but we are also raised into the world as God's body, so that our embodiment after death becomes pancosmic rather than acosmic. Because we are raised into the world and because the world is taken up into God, we are raised into God. Individual destiny and universal destiny are wrapped up together. We obtain some sense of what this might mean from the resurrection of Jesus, whose personal identity is preserved by his presence in and to the community that becomes his body, and which he empowers to become a liberated communion of free subjects. Then, when all things are subjected to him, he too will be subjected to God, so that God may be "all in all" (1 Cor. 15:28).

These few highly speculative things that can be said about resurrection draw us back to the theme of spiritual community—a communion of saints past, present, and future, which links us with predecessors and successors as well as contemporaries. Our appropriate concern is with how this community manifests itself today. It takes shape in many religious and quasi-religious places: not just Christian churches but Jewish synagogues, Buddhist temples, Muslim mosques, Latin American base communities, inter-religious dialogues, community organizations, movements struggling for human rights and ecojustice. Institutions are necessary but often also stifling.

The Christian churches in North America today find themselves in a state of crisis. Preoccupied with issues of authority, tradition, gender, and sexuality, they have lost a sense of mission, purpose, and identity. Mainline Protestant denominations seem to consume themselves in internecine conflicts. Systematic blockages in communication have eviscerated their spirituality. The salt of the Gospel has lost its savor at the very time that the world needs to hear the Gospel of Christ as never before. Other religions struggle with their own internal conflicts that block their messages and distort their practices. Perhaps realignments will come about to open up new possibilities oriented to the serious global issues of our time.

At the beginning of the third millennium, we know that we must pray for the coming of the Spirit and a new age of the Spirit, but prayer alone is not enough. If we act as though it is happening, it will begin to happen. It is a possible dream.

EXERCISES

1. Do you agree with the claim (found at the end of chapter 5, and repeated in chapter 6) that the Spirit precedes, accompanies, and follows the Son, that the reach of the Spirit exceeds that of the Son, and that the Spirit brings Christian theology into closer connection with other religious traditions than does the Son? Does such a statement not seem to pit pneumatology against Christology, giving the Spirit a privileged position vis-à-vis the Son? Try role playing in which you explore the complex relationship between the second and third "roles" of the Trinity.

2. Use a concordance to track down occurrences of the images of air (breath, wind), fire, light, and water (fountain) in the Bible. In

your judgment, how many of these are allusions to God's Spirit? What picture begins to emerge of how God interacts with the world?

3. The second section of the chapter (pp. 136–145) develops a theology of the Spirit by using the concepts of energy, relationality, and emergence. Does this make sense to you, or do you see it as fundamentally alien to the traditional doctrine of the Holy Spirit? Address this question by writing a brief, two-page version of your own theology of the Spirit. Share what you have written with other members of the group, and discuss the critical issues that you find yourselves confronting.

4. This book argues that the Spirit proceeds from a plurality of saving shapes of divine presence, not from Christ alone. What (if anything) protects such a view from an uncritical spiritualism, an inability to distinguish between demonic and divine forms of spirituality? Can Christians really believe that the Holy Spirit is also the Spirit of Buddha, Confucius, Socrates, Muhammad, Gandhi, to name but a few? How do we know that the demon that possessed Hitler is not a divine spirit?

5. Try your hand at creating an ecological spirituality, or a justice-oriented spirituality, or a pluralist spirituality. Your effort could take the form of a traditional essay, a poem or prayer, a service of worship, an artwork or video, an action strategy, a meditation on nature, a dialogue with an adherent of another faith, a website. Work individually or collaboratively. Ask what it is that is spiritual about what you have created. Share your efforts with others.

6. "Living in the community of the Spirit, we find ourselves beyond accusation and consolation" (p. 152). What does this mean, and does it make any sense? If the accusatory dimension is removed from religion, does not religion lose its effectiveness, its ability to control by authority and to threaten with eternal damnation? If the consolatory dimension is removed from religion, does not religion lose its ability to compensate for present sufferings and to promise eternal life? In the real world, we need threats and compensations, punishments and rewards. Human beings live by "miracle, mystery, and authority," said the Grand Inquisitor in Dostoyevsky's *The Brothers Karamazov*. The community of the Spirit is a utopian ideal. Discuss this with your classmates.

7. Read the novel *Adam Bede* by George Eliot, and reflect on how it relates to the issues discussed in this chapter (and to exercise 6 in particular). Is something like "redemptive transformation" taking place in this story? How?

8. What does the consummation of all things in God have to do with what happens in the world on a daily basis?

9. Is personal identity preserved after death? If so, how and in what form? Is this an unanswerable question, one that is irrelevant to an authentic life of faith?

10. What might call forth a spiritual awakening in our time, a communion of friends, prophets, and saints? Is such talk quaint nonsense in the age of self-help and information technology? (Exercises 8–10, which deal with different aspects of the puzzling topic of eschatology, might each be assigned to a different subgroup, with the subgroups in turn reporting to the whole class.)

11. Is the age of the Spirit an impossible dream?

Retake the quiz in exercise 1, chapter 1.

Glossary

Listed below are definitions of a number of terms, taking into account the way they are used in this book. For a fuller treatment of key terms, refer to the theological dictionaries listed in the bibliography for chapter 2.

adoptionism. The doctrine that Jesus of Nazareth was adopted as the Messiah or Son of God at some point in his life or after his death and resurrection.

agnosticism. The belief that God cannot be known or that judgments as to whether God exists cannot be made.

Alexandrine theologians. Cyril of Alexandria and other theologians of the fourth and fifth centuries who helped to establish the orthodox Logos-flesh Christology.

alienation. A disruption of relationships as a result of incompatibilities (benign sense) or of violation and victimization (malignant sense).

alterity. That which is other than or different from oneself.

Apologists. A group of second-century theologians who sought to articulate and defend the Christian faith in Greek and Roman culture.

apophatic theology. See "negative theology."

aseity. The quality of being self-caused or from oneself.

atheism. The doctrine that God does not exist or is an illusion.

atonement. See "substitionary atonement."

basileia. The Greek word for "kingdom."

being. The energy, power, or letting-be by which everything that is exists.

beings. Entities that exist in virtue of the power of being and that are constituted by relationships.

bondage of the will. The loss of freedom of choice, for example, of the freedom not to sin.

canon. An officially defined and approved body of writings or laws, for example, the writings included in the Hebrew Bible and the New Testament.

Chalcedon. A church council in 451 C.E., which established the orthodox doctrine that Christ was composed of two natures, divine and human, united in one person.

chaos. That which is unformed, indeterminate, contingent.

Christ (Messiah). The one anointed to be the king or deliverer of Israel, identified by Christians with Jesus of Nazareth as the definitive revelation and presence of God.

christocentric. Centered or focused on Christ.

Christology. The doctrine or study of Christ.

christomorphic. Having the shape or form of Christ.

compassion. A very strong form of love that takes the pathos and suffering of another into itself.

conceptualization. A reflective process by which symbols are raised to thought and metaphors are brought together into a more comprehensive frame of reference.

consciousness. The condition of being able to feel and think; being aware of oneself as a feeling, thinking, acting being related to other beings.

constructive theology. A form of systematic theology that emphasizes its humanly constructed character.

consummation. The end, completion, perfection of all things in God.

correlation, theology of. A theology that critically connects or correlates religious truths (answers) with cultural forms (questions), seeking both the intelligibility of religion and the transformation of culture; a method associated with Paul Tillich.

cosmology. A study, scientific or philosophical, of the nature of the world as a whole, the universe.

cosmotheandric. The interplay of God, the world, and humanity in a nexus of relationships, a holistic system.

crucifixion. A torturous form of execution practiced by the Romans and other ancient peoples; the death of Jesus on a cross.

culture. The social world or civilization constructed by a group of people over time.

deconstruction. A movement in philosophy and literary criticism that emphasizes the constructed character of all human knowledge and that seeks to take apart earlier constructions to expose their assumptions, fallacies, oppressions, and blindnesses.

dialectical. A way of thinking that sees both sides of an issue or finds a mediating position among differences; a method of question and answer that recognizes there are no final answers or conclusive formulations.

docetism. The doctrine that Jesus Christ was a god in human disguise who only appeared to be human.

doctrines. Teachings, especially of a philosophical, religious, or theological character; the principal Christian teachings about God, creation, humanity, sin and evil, Christ, redemption, church, consummation, Spirit.

dogma. An important teaching that is regarded as authoritative and officially sanctioned.

dogmatic theology, dogmatics. A system of theology that claims to set forth officially sanctioned, authoritative, and/or revealed truths (or dogmas).

ecclesial community. The Christian community of faith, the institutional form of which is the church.

ecclesiocentric. Centered or focused on the church.

ecclesiology. A study of the nature and activities of the church.

ecology. A study of the interdependence of living and nonliving systems on earth or in the entire cosmos.

economic Trinity. The threefold pattern of God's creative, redemptive, and consummating work in the world.

economy. God's plan of salvation or care for the world; the management of a household, business, society, or environment.

empathy. Sharing in the suffering or experience of another.

energy. That which is at work in the world as its fundamental dynamism.

Enlightenment. See "modernity."

entropy. The depletion of usable energy in a thermodynamic system.

eros. Desire or longing for union with an other; sexual love.

eschatology. Teaching about last things, the consummation of all things in God.

estrangement. See "alienation."

ethics. A study of the principles and policies that guide the practices of a religious faith or a society.

ethnocentrism. A centering or focusing on one's own ethnic group to the exclusion or derogation of other groups.

evil. The cosmic and social objectification of the effects of sin, rendering them more destructive and intransigent; a drift toward futility in nature.

experience. The matrix from which religious faiths arise, ranging from the root, revelatory experiences constitutive of a faith-tradition to individual and personal experiences.

faith. An immediate, participatory apprehension of truth, as well as a knowledge mediated by trustworthy persons, texts, testimonies, communities; a knowing founded on and oriented to a revelatory experience that grasps and shapes it.

fall. The transition from a state of innocence to a state of guilt or sin (represented mythologically in the Bible by the story of Adam and Eve).

fallibility, fragility. The susceptibility of human beings to failure, fault, sin.

figure. A form or shape (of speech, of action, of a body, of a person).

final cause. A causality that works by offering an invitation, goal, or lure.

finite. That which has limits or is limited by something other than itself.

first cause. A causality that works by initiating a chain of effects.

flight. As a form of sin: an escape from responsibility, submission to degrading conditions, longing for death or oblivion.

formal cause. A causality that works by providing a form or ideal for the shaping of events.

foundational theology. A branch of theology that examines the foundations of knowledge of God in the natural world and/or human experience.

freedom. Being in and for self through being in and for others; interdependent self-determination; participation in a community of friends and equals.

fundamentalism. A theological orientation that holds to a literal reading of an inerrant scripture and the acceptance of doctrinal formulations regarded as fundamental to salvation.

gestalt. A German loan word designating a shape, structure, or pattern that forms an identity composed of parts or differences; an integrated structure.

grace. A freely given gift, favor, or act of good will (for instance, God's redemptive or saving grace).

hedonism. The doctrine that happiness is the chief goal of human activity.

hermeneutics. The science or principles of interpretation (the "hermeneutical circle" points to the fact that every interpretation presupposes something that is given and that therefore all knowledge is circular).

hierarchy. A graded rank of ruling authority that claims to be based on a sacred or inviolate order.

historical theology. A study of the texts, traditions, and other cultural media by which the faith of a religious community has been given expression in the past.

holism. A way of understanding God, the world, and humanity as organically related, composing a differentiated unity.

homophobia. Fear of or revulsion toward homosexuality.

hypostasis. An essence, substance, functioning entity, or identifying principle (in the trinitarian debates, it referred to the three divine persons; in the christological debates, it referred to the person of the divine Logos incarnate in Jesus of Nazareth).

idealism. A philosophical school that holds that ideas (concepts, forms) constitute the fundamental reality of things.

ideology. A theory or idea that contributes to a social practice; the rationalization of an unjust practice by an uncritical, often emotional or irrational belief.

idolatry. Worshiping something finite as though it were God; attempting to secure the human condition through attachment to false foundations and mundane goods.

imagination. The process of forming mental images by which new possibilities and combinations of reality are envisioned; creative thinking.

immanent. That which functions within itself or is present in something else.

immanent Trinity. The threefold pattern of God's self-relatedness prior to and apart from the world and its creation.

immutability. The doctrine that God does not change.

incarnation. Literally, entering into flesh or bodily form; figuratively, God's taking on human form in an individual figure such as Jesus of Nazareth.

incarnationism. The doctrine that the Son of God or divine Logos constituted the personal identity (the persona or hypostasis) of Jesus of Nazareth.

inclusive Trinity. God's internal self-relatedness together with God's creative-redemptive and consummating work in the world.

infinite. That which is limitless, over-reaching or including everything that is finite.

injustice. The disruption and distortion of just or right relationships; withholding from an entity that which is necessary for its flourishing or well-being.

interhuman, interpersonal. See "intersubjective."

interpretation. A process of understanding what is given by tradition or experience through procedures of criticism, explanation, appropriation, appreciation.

intersubjective, intersubjectivity. A nexus of inter-related subjects or persons, which may or may not assume institutional form.

involuntary. That aspect of the human being that is not subject to volitional acts but rather is given by nature.

justice. A situation in which right relationships (fair, impartial, mutually supportive) prevail among human beings; a practice of giving to each being what belongs to it or is due to it for the sake of its perfection.

Kabala. A form of medieval Jewish teaching based on a mystical interpretation of scriptures.

kataphatic theology. See "positive theology."

kenoticism. The doctrine that the incarnate Logos emptied itself of its divine qualities and assumed human form in Jesus of Nazareth.

kingdom of God. The central image found in Jesus' sayings and parables, describing metaphorically the effects of God's redemptive activity in the world.

law. An instruction or rule for fair and consistent practices; an instrument of suppression, control, judgment.

liberal theology. A theological movement beginning with Friedrich Schleiermacher, which attempted to reformulate traditional Christian claims in light of modern culture and critical scholarship; "revisionary" liberalism shares postmodern critiques of modern culture but attempts to continue the liberal project.

liberation theologies. Theologies written from the perspective of oppressed or marginalized peoples and groups (women, African Americans, Hispanics, Latin Americans, Asians, Africans, gays, and lesbians), which stress the centrality of liberation or emancipation to the Christian gospel.

logocentric. Centered or focused on language or on the divine Logos.

Logos. The Greek term for "word," "speech"; the Word by which God reveals godself in the world and acts creatively and redemptively; a persona of the Trinity.

metaphor. A figure of speech by which meaning is transferred between two or more initially quite different things, or by which one thing stands for another thing, or by which the connection between things is poetically or intuitively grasped.

metaphysics. The branch of philosophy that deals with first principles and seeks to explain the nature of being or reality (ontology) and the origin and structure of the world (cosmology).

miracle. A direct divine action in the world, which interrupts natural processes.

modernity. A period in Western culture beginning with the rise of natural science in the seventeenth century and of critical scholarship in the eighteenth and nineteenth centuries (the "Enlightenment").

mystery (of God). That ultimate reality that is hidden from view and is not comprehensible in human terms, but that manifests a higher intelligibility.

mysticism. A form of religious experience that regards God as an incomprehensible mystery, yet believes that it is possible to achieve communion with God through contemplation and spiritual discipline.

myth, mythology. A way of thinking about the origin and end of the world, divine creativity, and/or God's being and activity in terms of stories and relationships that are represented as historical fact but are the product of human imagination.

negative (apophatic) theology. A theological tradition that denies the possibility of knowing or speaking about God in any positive, determinate sense; we know only what God is not, not what God is.

Nicene Creed. A creed adopted at the Council of Nicea, 325 C.E., establishing the orthodox doctrine of the Trinity.

nihilism. The view that life has no purpose and is oriented to sheer nothingness or absurdity.

ontology. A philosophical study of being or reality.

ontotheology. A type of theology that makes claims about the being, substance, or reality status of God or that regards being-itself as intrinsically divine or infinite.

openness. The capacity of a human being to enter into relationship with ultimate reality or God.

organism. A complex dynamic system whose parts work together interactively.

paideia. A Greek term meaning "nurture" or "education"; the formation of character through the acquisition of practical wisdom.

panentheism. The doctrine that all things subsist or have their being in God, but are not identical with God.

pantheism. The doctrine that all things are God (acosmic pantheism) or that God is identical with everything that is (atheistic pantheism).

parables. Stories told by Jesus, which metaphorically describe how God acts in the world.

Paraclete. A traditional name for the Holy Spirit as comforter and advocate.

paradigm. A model or example.

paradox. Something that appears contrary to reason or evidence but that reveals a deeper truth.

patriarchy. The rule exercised by dominant males ("the fathers").

patristic age. The age of the so-called fathers of church doctrine, from the second through the sixth centuries.

pedagogy. The activity of a teacher, leader, or instructor; an early model for understanding the redemptive work of Christ.

person. A human being who exercises responsibility through relationships to self and others; an "I" or self-consciousness.

persona/ae. A Latin term meaning a functioning entity engaged in a role or action; a character.

personeity. The highest or most intense form of personhood (a term coined by S. T. Coleridge).

philosophical theology. An interpretation of the claims of a religious or faith tradition in more general philosophical categories.

pneumatocentric. Centered or focused on the Spirit.

pneumatology. The doctrine or study of the (Holy) Spirit.

positive (kataphatic) theology. A theological tradition that affirms the possibility of explicit knowledge of God, usually on the basis of divine revelation or self-disclosure.

postliberal theology. A theological movement critical of the alleged accommodation of Protestant liberalism to the principles of modern culture; emphasizes the importance of maintaining the identity of confessional traditions.

postmodernity. A period beginning in the late twentieth century when the cultural consensus known as modernity began to break down.

practical theology. A study of the way in which the faith of a religious community is appropriated, enacted, and practiced.

pragmatism. A philosophical school that analyzes meaning principally in terms of practices or uses (how an idea is used determines what it means).

praxis. The Greek word for "action," especially human action of a cultural or linguistic character.

Priestly and Yahwist accounts. Two of the literary sources or strands making up the first five books of the Hebrew Bible.

prophet. A person who brings critical judgment to bear on present conditions and envisions a better future.

providence. God's preservation and ordering of the world toward an end.

provincialism. An attitude that is limited and narrow, not open to other provinces of meaning and experience.

quantum theory. The theory that energy radiates in subatomic units (quanta) that take the form of both waves and particles.

radical orthodoxy. A theological movement (mostly among High Church Anglicans) that combines a radical critique of society with an orthodox Catholic metaphysics.

redemption. The process of being transformed toward some good or fulfillment; a liberation or emancipation from whatever holds persons in bondage; for Christians, brought about by God acting in and through Christ and the Spirit; compare "salvation."

relativism. The view that because all knowledge is relative to context nothing can be known of the true nature or purpose of things.

relativity, relationality. The fundamental character of the universe as interconnected, fluid, changing.

religious pluralism. The acknowledgment of a diversity of religious traditions arising in different cultural contexts, and the acceptance of a rough equivalence between them so that none can rightfully claim to be intellectually and morally superior to another.

resurrection. The surging forth again of life from death; the belief or experience that the crucified Jesus is spiritually alive and at work in the world.

revelation. An unveiling or disclosure of what is hidden or mysterious.

saints. Those who have been sanctified, made holy, by the grace of Christ through the power of the Holy Spirit; especially good and righteous persons who become models of Christian life.

salvation. A process of healing or making whole, brought about (for Christians) by God through Jesus Christ; compare "redemption."

scripture. The sacred, originating texts of a religious tradition, often thought to be directly inspired by God.

serendipitous creativity. The idea that creativity leads to fortunate or beneficial outcomes through an accidental or contingent process.

sin. A disruption of the human condition caused by the violation of relationships (to God, the world, and fellow human beings).

Sophia. The Greek name for God's Wisdom.

Spirit. That which is alive, active, energetic, moving, fluid, relational, and in its highest forms rational, conscious, intelligible; for Christians, the most adequate term for understanding God's inner dynamism and for designating God's creative, redemptive, and consummating activity in the world.

spirituality. Life in and by the power of the Spirit.

subject. A self-aware agent capable of initiating and receiving actions.

substance. The being, essence, or reality that underlies or infuses all that is.

substitutionary atonement. The doctrine that the God-man Jesus Christ pays the penalty for sin in place of or as a substitute for human beings, satisfying the divine demand for justice and thus bringing about a reconciliation between God and humanity.

supernaturalism. The belief that God miraculously intervenes in natural processes to bring about special results.

surrealism. Realism intensified or exaggerated to the point of disclosing something new, unexpected, shocking.

symbol. A word, image, or metaphor that stands for or represents something that cannot be directly or simply expressed (all religious language is symbolic in this sense).

systematic theology. A comprehensive overview and interpretation of the various topics or doctrines of theology, especially in terms of their connections and interdependence.

telos. A goal or purpose.

tetragrammaton. The divine name revealed in Exod. 3:14, YHWH, left unpronounced by Jews, sometimes pronounced "Yahweh" by Christians, or written as a circumlocution, "The Lord."

theological anthropology. A study of the nature and activity of human beings as created by God, fallen into sin, and redeemed through Christ.

theology. Literally, language or thought about God; more generally, disciplined reflection on the meaning and truth of the contents of a religious faith.

tradition. The interpretation and handing on of a received body of scriptures or teachings; more generally, the ongoing historical development of a religion.

tragedy. A condition, common to the finite world in its contingency and freedom, in which the possibility of good necessarily allows for the possibility of evil.

transcendent. That which stands beyond something else and is not limited by it.

Trinity. The doctrine that God, though one and indivisible, subsists in three personae or modes of being, traditionally named Father, Son, and Holy Spirit.

triune configuration. The interplay of the figures or personae that constitute the being and act of God.

Wisdom of God. A figure or shape of God's spiritual presence in the world by which redemption is brought about, analogous to the divine Word or Logos, but with distinctive qualities that relate to wisdom as a practical form of knowledge.

Word of God. A form or modality in which God communicates god-self in the world; sometimes identified with Christ, scripture, and/or preaching.

xenophobia. Fear or hatred of what is other or different.

Bibliography

Sources for This Book
and Suggestions for Further Reading

Earlier works by the author that have contributed to the writing of this book:

Jesus—Word and Presence: An Essay in Christology. Philadelphia: Fortress Press, 1971.

New Birth of Freedom: A Theology of Bondage and Liberation. Philadelphia: Fortress Press, 1976.

Revisioning the Church: Ecclesial Freedom in the New Paradigm. Philadelphia: Fortress Press, 1988.

God in History: Shapes of Freedom. Nashville: Abingdon Press, 1989.

Winds of the Spirit: A Constructive Christian Theology. Louisville: Westminster John Knox Press, 1994. London: SCM Press, 1994. The present work draws substantially from this book.

G. W. F. Hegel: Theologian of the Spirit. Minneapolis: Fortress Press, 1997. Edinburgh: T. and T. Clark, 1997.

God's Wisdom: Toward a Theology of Education. Louisville: Westminster John Knox Press, 1999.

Theology in the Fiction of George Eliot: The Mystery beneath the Real. London: SCM Press, 2001. Minneapolis: Fortress Press, 2001.

An asterisk indicates books listed below that are especially appropriate for beginning students of theology.

Chapter 1. A New Millennium

*Berry, Thomas. *The Dream of the Earth*. San Francisco: Sierra Club Books, 1988.

Birch, Charles, William Eakin, and Jay B. McDaniel, eds. *Liberating Life: Contemporary Approaches to Ecological Theology*. Maryknoll, N.Y.: Orbis Books, 1990.

Cobb, John B., Jr. *Transforming Christianity and the World: A Way beyond Absolutism and Relativism*. Ed. and intro. Paul F. Knitter. Maryknoll, N.Y.: Orbis Books, 1999.

Cone, James H. *God of the Oppressed*. New York: Seabury Press, 1975.

D'Costa, Gavin, ed. *The Myth of a Pluralistic Theology of Religions*. Maryknoll, N.Y.: Orbis Books, 1990.

Gutiérrez, Gustavo. *A Theology of Liberation: History, Politics, and Salvation*. 15th anniversary ed., trans. and ed. Caridad Inda and John Eagleson. Maryknoll, N.Y.: Orbis Books, 1988.

*Hick, John. *A Christian Theology of Religions: The Rainbow of Faiths*. Louisville: Westminster John Knox Press, 1995.

Hick, John, and Paul F. Knitter, eds. *The Myth of Christian Uniqueness: Toward a Pluralistic Theology of Religions*. Maryknoll, N.Y.: Orbis Books, 1987.

Knitter, Paul F. *No Other Name? A Critical Survey of Christian Attitudes toward the World Religions*. Maryknoll, N.Y.: Orbis Books, 1985.

*_____. *One Earth, Many Religions: Multifaith Dialogue and Global Responsibility*. Maryknoll, N.Y.: Orbis Books, 1995.

*McFague, Sallie. *Super, Natural Christians: How We Should Love Nature*. Minneapolis: Fortress Press, 1997.

Niebuhr, H. Richard. *Theology, History, and Culture*. Ed. William Stacy Johnson. New Haven: Yale University Press, 1996.

Pieris, Aloysius. *An Asian Theology of Liberation*. Maryknoll, N.Y.: Orbis Books, 1988.

*Ruether, Rosemary Radford. *Gaia and God: An Ecofeminist Theology of Earth Healing*. San Francisco: HarperSanFrancisco, 1992.

Tillich, Paul. *The Courage to Be*. New Haven: Yale University Press, 1952.

Troeltsch, Ernst. *Christian Thought: Its History and Application*. Trans. and ed. Baron F. von Hügel. London: University of London Press, 1923.

*Ward, Keith. *God, Faith and the New Millennium: Christian Belief in an Age of Science*. Oxford: Oneworld Publications, 1998.

Chapter 2. Thinking Theologically

Barth, Karl. *Church Dogmatics*. Ed. G. W. Bromiley and T. F. Torrance. Vol. 1: *The Doctrine of the Word of God*. Edinburgh: T. and T. Clark, 1936, 1956.

Browning, Don S., ed. *Practical Theology*. San Francisco: Harper and Row, 1983.

Calvin, John. *Institutes of the Christian Religion*. Trans. Ford Lewis Battles. Philadelphia: Westminster Press, 1960.

*Chopp, Rebecca S., and Mark Lewis Taylor, eds. *Reconstructing Christian Theology*. Minneapolis: Fortress Press, 1994.

Dillenberger, John. *God Hidden and Revealed*. Philadelphia: Muhlenberg Press, 1953.

Ebeling, Gerhard. *The Problem of Historicity in the Church and Its Proclamation*. Trans. Grover Foley. Philadelphia: Fortress Press, 1966.

_____. *The Study of Theology*. Trans. Duane A. Priebe. Philadelphia: Fortress Press, 1978.

_____. *Word and Faith*. Trans. James W. Leitch. Philadelphia: Fortress Press, 1963.

Evans, James H. *We Have Been Believers: An African-American Systematic Theology*. Minneapolis: Fortress Press, 1992.

Farley, Edward. *Ecclesial Reflection: An Anatomy of Theological Method*. Philadelphia: Fortress Press, 1982.

_____. *Theologia: The Fragmentation and Unity of Theological Education*. Philadelphia: Fortress Press, 1983.

Fiorenza, Francis Schüssler. *Foundational Theology: Jesus and the Church*. New York: Crossroad, 1984.

Fiorenza, Francis Schüssler, and John P. Galvin, eds. *Systematic Theology: Roman Catholic Perspectives*. 2 vols. Minneapolis: Fortress Press, 1991.

Ford, David F., ed. *The Modern Theologians: An Introduction to Christian Theology in the Twentieth Century*. 2d ed. 2 vols. Oxford: Basil Blackwell, 1997.

*_____. *Theology: A Very Short Introduction*. New York: Oxford University Press, 1999.

Gadamer, Hans-Georg. *Truth and Method*. 2d ed. Rev. trans. Joel Weinsheimer and Donald G. Marshall. New York: Crossroad, 1989.

Gerrish, B. A. *Saving and Secular Faith: An Invitation to Systematic Theology*. Minneapolis: Fortress Press, 1999.

*Gilkey, Langdon. *Message and Existence: An Introduction to Christian Theology*. New York: Seabury Press, 1980.

Gill, Robin, ed. *Readings in Modern Theology: Britain and America*. Nashville: Abingdon Press, 1995.

Hall, John Douglas. *Christian Theology in a North American Context*. Vol. 1: *Thinking the Faith*. Vol. 2: *Professing the Faith*. Minneapolis: Fortress Press, 1991, 1993.

Heidegger, Martin. *On the Way to Language*. Trans. Peter D. Hertz. New York: Harper and Row, 1971.

_____. *Poetry, Language, Thought*. Trans. Albert Hofstadter. New York: Harper and Row, 1971.

*Hodgson, Peter C., and Robert H. King, eds. *Christian Theology: An Introduction to Its Traditions and Tasks*. 3d ed. Minneapolis: Fortress Press, 1994.

*_____. *Readings in Christian Theology*. Minneapolis: Fortress Press, 1985.

Jeanrond, Werner G. *Theological Hermeneutics: Development and Significance.* New York: Crossroad, 1991.

*Jones, Gareth. *Christian Theology: A Brief Introduction*. Malden, Mass.: Blackwell Publishers, 1999.

Kaufman, Gordon D. *In the Face of Mystery: A Constructive Theology*. Cambridge, Mass.: Harvard University Press, 1993.

Kelsey, David H. *To Understand God Truly: What's Theological about a Theological School?* Louisville: Westminster John Knox Press, 1992.

_____. *The Uses of Scripture in Recent Theology*. Philadelphia: Fortress Press, 1975.

Macquarrie, John. *Principles of Christian Theology*. New York: Charles Scribner's Sons, 1966.

McFague, Sallie. *Life Abundant: Rethinking Theology and Economy for a Planet in Peril*. Minneapolis: Fortress Press, 2001.

*_____. *Models of God: Theology for an Ecological, Nuclear Age*. Philadelphia: Fortress Press, 1987.

*McGrath, Alister. *Christian Theology: An Introduction*. Oxford: Oxford University Press, 1994.

*Migliore, Daniel. *Faith Seeking Understanding: An Introduction to Christian Theology*. Grand Rapids: Wm. B. Eerdmans, 1991.

Morse, Christopher. *Not Every Spirit: A Dogmatics of Christian Disbelief*. Valley Forge, Pa.: Trinity Press International, 1994.

*Musser, Donald W., and Joseph L. Price, eds. *A New Handbook of Christian Theologians*. Nashville: Abingdon Press, 1996.

*_____. *A New Handbook of Christian Theology*. Nashville: Abingdon Press, 1992.

*Neville, Robert C. *A Theology Primer.* Albany: State University of New York Press, 1991.

Niebuhr, H. Richard. *Faith on Earth: An Inquiry into the Structure of Human Faith*. Ed. Richard R. Niebuhr. New Haven: Yale University Press, 1989.

_____. *The Meaning of Revelation*. New York: Macmillan, 1941.

*Norris, Kathleen. *Amazing Grace: A Vocabulary of Faith*. New York: Riverhead Books, 1998.

Rahner, Karl. *Foundations of Christian Faith: An Introduction to the Idea of Christianity*. Trans. William V. Dych. New York: Crossroad, 1978.

*Richardson, Alan, and John Bowden, eds. *The Westminster Dictionary of Christian Theology*. Philadelphia: Westminster Press, 1983.

Ricoeur, Paul. *From Text to Action: Essays in Hermeneutics, II*. Trans. Kathleen Blamey and John B. Thompson. Evanston: Northwestern University Press, 1991.

_____. *Hermeneutics and the Human Sciences*. Trans. John B. Thompson. Cambridge: Cambridge University Press, 1981.

_____. *Interpretation Theory*. Fort Worth: Texas Christian University, 1976.

Ruether, Rosemary Radford. *Sexism and God-Talk: Toward a Feminist Theology*. Boston: Beacon Press, 1993.

Schleiermacher, Friedrich. *The Christian Faith*. Ed. H. R. Mackintosh and J. S. Stewart. Edinburgh: T. and T. Clark, 1928.

Smart, Ninian, and Steven Konstantine. *Christian Systematic Theology in a World Context*. Minneapolis: Fortress Press, 1991.

*Sölle, Dorothee. *Thinking about God: An Introduction to Theology*. Philadelphia: Trinity Press International, 1990.

*Stone, Howard W., and James O. Duke. *How to Think Theologically*. Minneapolis: Fortress Press, 1996.

Taylor, Mark C. *Erring: A Postmodern A/theology*. Chicago: University of Chicago Press, 1984.

*Thistlethwaite, Susan Brooks, and Mary Potter Engel, eds. *Lift Every Voice: Constructing Christian Theologies from the Underside*. Rev. ed. Maryknoll, N.Y.: Orbis Books, 1998.

Tillich, Paul. *Systematic Theology*. Vol. 1: Introduction and Part 1, Reason and Revelation. Chicago: University of Chicago Press, 1951.

Tracy, David. *Blessed Rage for Order: The New Pluralism in Theology*. New York: Seabury Press, 1975.

_____. *Plurality and Ambiguity: Hermeneutics, Religion, Hope*. San Francisco: Harper and Row, 1987.

*Williamson, Clark M. *Way of Blessing, Way of Life: A Christian Theology*. St. Louis: Chalice Press, 1999.

Chapter 3. God and the World

Aquinas, Thomas. *Summa theologiae*, vol. 6: *The Trinity*. Ed. Ceslaus Velecky. London: Blackfriars, 1965.

Augustine, Saint. *On the Trinity*. In vol. 2 of *Basic Writings of Saint Augustine*, ed. Whitney J. Oates. New York: Random House, 1948.

Barbour, Ian. *Religion in an Age of Science*. San Francisco: Harper and Row, 1990.

Barth, Karl. *Church Dogmatics*. Vol. 2: *The Doctrine of God*. Ed. G. W. Bromiley and T. F. Torrance. Edinburgh: T. and T. Clark, 1957.

Birch, Charles, and John B. Cobb Jr. *The Liberation of Life: From the Cell to the Community*. Cambridge: Cambridge University Press, 1981.

Cobb, John B., Jr. *A Christian Natural Theology: Based on the Thought of Alfred North Whitehead*. Philadelphia: Westminster Press, 1965.

* _____. *God and the World*. Philadelphia: Westminster Press, 1969.

Davies, Paul. *God and the New Physics*. New York: Simon and Schuster, 1983.

Farley, Edward. *Divine Empathy: A Theology of God*. Minneapolis: Fortress Press, 1996.

Gilkey, Langdon. *Reaping the Whirlwind: A Christian Interpretation of History*. New York: Seabury Press, 1976.

Gleick, James. *Chaos: Making a New Science*. New York: Penguin Books, 1987.

Hegel, Georg Wilhelm Friedrich. *The Encyclopedia Logic*. Trans. T. F. Geraets, W. A. Suchting, and H. S. Harris. Indianapolis: Hackett, 1991.

_____. *Lectures on the Philosophy of Religion.* 3 vols. Trans. and ed. Peter C. Hodgson et al. Berkeley and Los Angeles: University of California Press, 1984, 1985, 1987.

_____. *Phenomenology of Spirit.* Trans. J. B. Baillie. London: Allen and Unwin, 1949.

Heidegger, Martin. *Being and Time.* Trans. Joan Stambaugh. Albany: State University of New York Press, 1996.

Jantzen, Grace. *God's World, God's Body.* Philadelphia: Westminster Press, 1984.

*Johnson, Elizabeth. *She Who Is: The Mystery of God in Feminist Theological Discourse.* New York: Crossroad, 1992.

Jüngel, Eberhard. *God as the Mystery of the World: On the Foundation of the Theology of the Crucified One in the Dispute between Theism and Atheism.* Trans. Darrell L. Guder. Grand Rapids: Wm. B. Eerdmans, 1983.

*Kelly, J. N. D. *Early Christian Doctrines.* London: Adam and Charles Black, 1958. Chapters 4-5, 10.

*McFague, Sallie. *The Body of God: An Ecological Theology.* Minneapolis: Fortress Press, 1993.

Moltmann, Jürgen. *The Trinity and the Kingdom of God.* Trans. Margaret Kohl. San Francisco: Harper and Row, 1981.

Monod, Jacques. *Chance and Necessity: An Essay on the Natural Philosophy of Modern Biology.* New York: Vintage Books, 1971.

Pailin, David A. *God and the Processes of Reality: Foundations of a Credible Theism.* London and New York: Routledge, 1989.

Pannikar, Raimundo. *The Cosmotheandric Experience: Emerging Religious Consciousness.* Maryknoll, N.Y.: Orbis Books, 1993.

Peacocke, Arthur. *Creation and the World of Science.* Oxford: Clarendon Press, 1979.

_____. *Theology for a Scientific Age.* Oxford: Basil Blackwell, 1990.

Peters, Ted, ed. *Cosmos as Creation: Theology and Science in Consonance.* Nashville: Abingdon Press, 1989.

*Polkinghorne, John. *One World: The Interaction of Science and Theology.* Princeton: Princeton University Press, 1986.

_____. *Science and Providence: God's Interaction with the World.* Boston: Shambhala Publications, 1989.

Rahner, Karl. *Hearer of the Word: Laying the Foundation for a Philosophy of Religion.* Trans. of 1st ed. Joseph Donceel, ed. Andrew Tallon. New York: Continuum, 1994. The 2d ed., to which reference is made in the text, is *Hörer des Wortes: Zur Grundlegung einer Religionsphilosophie,* ed. J. B. Metz. Munich: Kösel-Verlag, 1963. An English translation of this edition exists but is very poor.

_____. *The Trinity.* Trans. Joseph Donceel. New York: Herder and Herder, 1970.

*Rusch, William G., ed. *The Trinitarian Controversy.* Philadelphia: Fortress Press, 1980.

*Swimme, Brian, and Thomas Berry. *The Universe Story.* San Francisco: HarperSanFrancisco, 1992.

*Suchocki, Marjorie Hewitt. *God, Christ, Church: A Practical Guide to Process Theology*. New York: Crossroad, 1986.

Tillich, Paul. *Systematic Theology*. Vol. 1: Part 2, Being and God. Chicago: University of Chicago Press, 1951.

Toulmin, Stephen. *The Return to Cosmology: Postmodern Science and the Theology of Nature*. Berkeley and Los Angeles: University of California Press, 1982.

Trefil, James J. *The Moment of Creation: Big Bang Physics from Before the First Millisecond to the Present Universe*. New York: Macmillan, 1983.

Troeltsch, Ernst. *The Christian Faith*. Trans. Garrett E. Paul. Minneapolis: Fortress Press, 1991.

Whitehead, Alfred North. *Process and Reality*. New York: Macmillan, 1929.

_____. *Religion in the Making*. New York: Macmillan, 1926.

*Wiles, Maurice. *God's Action in the World*. London: SCM Press, 1986.

Williams, Robert R. *Recognition: Fichte and Hegel on the Other*. Albany: State University of New York Press, 1992.

Chapter 4. Human Nature and Evil

For the first section of this chapter, see also the works on theology and nature listed under chapter 3.

Barth, Karl. *Church Dogmatics*. Vol. 3: *The Doctrine of Creation*. Ed. G. W. Bromiley and T. F. Torrance. Edinburgh: T. and T. Clark, 1958–61.

*Bonhoeffer, Dietrich. *Creation and Fall: A Theological Interpretation of Genesis 1–3*. London: SCM Press, 1959.

Bultmann, Rudolf. *Theology of the New Testament*. Trans. Kendrick Grobel. 2 vols. New York: Charles Scribner's Sons, 1954–55.

Farley, Edward. *Good and Evil: Interpreting a Human Condition*. Minneapolis: Fortress Press, 1990.

*Farley, Wendy. *Tragic Vision and Divine Compassion*. Louisville: Westminster John Knox Press, 1990.

Harris, Errol E. *Cosmos and Anthropos: A Philosophical Interpretation of the Anthropic Cosmological Principle*. Atlantic Highlands, N.J.: Humanities Press International, 1991.

Hegel, Georg Wilhelm Friedrich. *Philosophy of Right*. Trans. T. M. Knox. Oxford: Oxford University Press, 1952.

Kaufman, Gordon. *In Face of Mystery*. See bibliography for chapter 2.

Keller, Catherine. *The Face of the Deep: Theology at the Edge of Chaos*. Forthcoming.

Kierkegaard, Søren. *The Concept of Anxiety*. Ed. and trans. Reidar Thomte. Princeton: Princeton University Press, 1980.

_____. *The Sickness unto Death*. Ed. and trans. Howard V. Hong and Edna H. Hong. Princeton: Princeton University Press, 1980.

Levinas, Emmanuel. *Totality and Infinity: An Essay on Exteriority*. Trans. Alphonso Lingis. Pittsburgh: Duquesne University Press, 1969.

Niebuhr, H. Richard. *The Responsible Self: An Essay in Christian Moral Philosophy*. Intro. James M. Gustafson. New York: Harper and Row, 1963.

Niebuhr, Reinhold. *The Nature and Destiny of Man.* 2 vols. New York: Charles Scribner's Sons, 1941.

*Pannenberg, Wolfhart. *What Is Man? Contemporary Anthropology in Theological Perspective.* Philadelphia: Fortress Press, 1970.

Ricoeur, Paul. *Fallible Man: Philosophy of the Will.* Trans. Charles Kelbley. Chicago: Henry Regnery, 1967.

_____. *Freedom and Nature: The Voluntary and the Involuntary.* Trans. Erazim V. Kohák. Evanston: Northwestern University Press, 1966.

_____. *The Symbolism of Evil.* Trans. Emerson Buchanan. Boston: Beacon Press, 1969.

Sands, Kathleen M. *Escape from Paradise: Evil and Tragedy in Feminist Theology.* Minneapolis: Fortress Press, 1994.

*Suchocki, Marjorie Hewitt. *The Fall to Violence: Original Sin in Relational Theology.* New York: Continuum, 1994.

Tillich, Paul. *Systematic Theology.* Vol. 2: Existence and the Christ. Chicago: University of Chicago Press, 1957.

Chapter 5. Jesus and Redemption

Barth, Karl. *Church Dogmatics.* Vol. 4: *The Doctrine of Reconciliation.* Ed. G. W. Bromiley and T. F. Torrance. Edinburgh: T. and T. Clark, 1956–62.

Bonhoeffer, Dietrich. *Christ the Center.* Trans. John Bowden. New York: Harper and Row, 1966.

_____. *Letters and Papers from Prison.* See bibliography for chapter 6.

Brock, Rita Nakashima. *Journeys by Heart: A Christology of Erotic Power.* New York: Crossroad, 1988.

Bultmann, Rudolf. *Jesus Christ and Mythology.* New York: Charles Scribner's Sons, 1958.

Cobb, John B. Jr. *Christ in a Pluralistic Age.* Philadelphia: Westminster Press, 1975.

_____. *Transforming Christianity and the World.* See bibliography for chapter 1.

Davis, Stephen T., ed. *Encountering Jesus: A Debate on Christology.* Atlanta: John Knox Press, 1988.

Edwards, Denis. *Jesus the Wisdom of God: An Ecological Theology.* Maryknoll, N.Y.: Orbis Books, 1995.

Farley, Edward. *Divine Empathy.* See bibliography for chapter 3.

Frei, Hans W. *The Identity of Jesus Christ.* Philadelphia: Fortress Press, 1975.

Fuller, Reginald H. *Foundations of New Testament Christology.* New York: Charles Scribner's Sons, 1965.

Haight, Roger. *Jesus: Symbol of God.* Maryknoll, N.Y.: Orbis Books, 1999.

*Hick, John. *The Metaphor of God Incarnate: Christology in a Pluralistic Age.* Louisville: Westminster John Knox Press, 1993.

_____, ed. *The Myth of God Incarnate.* Philadelphia: Westminster Press, 1977.

*Käsemann, Ernst. *Jesus Means Freedom.* Trans. Frank Clarke. Philadelphia: Fortress Press, 1970.

*Kelly, J. N. D. *Early Christian Doctrines.* London: Adam and Charles Black, 1958. Chapters 6–7, 11–12, 14.

*Knitter, Paul F. *Jesus and the Other Names: Christian Mission and Global Responsibility.* Maryknoll, N.Y.: Orbis Books, 1996.

*Knox, John. *The Humanity and Divinity of Christ: A Study of Pattern in Christology.* Cambridge: Cambridge University Press, 1967.

Macquarrie, John. *Jesus Christ in Modern Thought.* Philadelphia: Trinity Press International, 1990.

Moltmann, Jürgen. *The Crucified God: The Cross of Christ as the Foundation and Criticism of Christian Theology.* Trans. R. A. Wilson and John Bowden. New York: Harper and Row, 1974.

*Norris, Richard A., ed. *The Christological Controversy.* Philadelphia: Fortress Press, 1980.

*Otatti, Douglas F. *Jesus Christ and Christian Vision.* Louisville: Westminster John Knox Press, 1989, 1996.

Panikkar, Raimundo. *The Unknown Christ of Hinduism: Toward an Ecumenical Christophany.* Rev. ed. Maryknoll: N.Y.: Orbis Books, 1981.

Rahner, Karl. *On the Theology of Death.* New York: Herder and Herder, 1965.

*Ruether, Rosemary Radford. *To Change the World: Christology and Cultural Criticism.* New York: Crossroad, 1983.

Schreiter, Robert J., ed. *Faces of Jesus in Africa.* Maryknoll, N.Y.: Orbis Books, 1991.

Schüssler Fiorenza, Elisabeth. *In Memory of Her: A Feminist Theological Reconstruction of Christian Origins.* New York: Crossroad, 1983.

————. *Jesus: Miriam's Child, Sophia's Prophet: Critical Issues in Feminist Christology.* New York: Continuum, 1994.

Sugirtharajah, R. S., ed. *Asian Faces of Jesus.* Maryknoll, N.Y.: Orbis Books, 1993.

Taylor, Mark K. *Remembering Esperanza: A Cultural-Political Theology for North American Praxis.* Maryknoll, N.Y.: Orbis Books, 1990.

Thangaraj, M. Thomas. *The Crucified Guru: An Experiment in Cross-Cultural Theology.* Nashville: Abingdon Press, 1994.

Chapter 6. The Age of the Spirit

See also the books listed under chapter 1.

Bonhoeffer, Dietrich. *Letters and Papers from Prison.* Ed. Eberhard Bethge. Trans. Reginald H. Fuller, et al. New York: Simon and Schuster, 1997.

Cobb, John B., and Christopher Ives, eds. *The Emptying God: A Buddhist-Jewish-Christian Conversation.* Maryknoll, N.Y.: Orbis Books, 1990.

*Comblin, José. *The Holy Spirit and Liberation.* Maryknoll, N.Y.: Orbis Books, 1989.

Forstman, Jack. *Christian Faith in Dark Times: Theological Conflicts in the Shadow of Hitler.* Louisville: Westminster John Knox Press, 1992.

*Gutiérrez, Gustavo. *The Power of the Poor in History.* Trans. Robert R. Barr. Maryknoll, N.Y.: Orbis Books, 1983.

*_____. *We Drink from Our Own Wells: The Spiritual Journey of a People.* Trans. Matthew J. O'Connell. Maryknoll, N.Y.: Orbis Books, 1984.

Hegel, Georg Wilhelm Friedrich. *Lectures on the Philosophy of World History. Introduction: Reason in History.* Trans. H. B. Nisbet. Cambridge: Cambridge University Press, 1975.

*Hendry, George. *The Holy Spirit in Christian Theology.* Philadelphia: Westminster Press, 1956.

*Hick, John. *The Fifth Dimension: An Exploration of the Spiritual Realm.* Oxford: Oneworld Publications, 1999.

Hood, Robert E. *Must God Remain Greek? Afro Cultures and God-Talk.* Minneapolis: Fortress Press, 1990.

*Johnson, Elizabeth A. *Friends of God and Prophets: A Feminist Theological Reading of the Communion of Saints.* New York: Continuum, 1998.

Keller, Catherine. *Apocalypse Now and Then: A Feminist Guide to the End of the World.* Boston: Beacon Press, 1996.

Kovel, Joel. *History and Spirit: An Inquiry into the Philosophy of Liberation.* Boston: Beacon Press, 1991.

Krieger, David J. *The New Universalism: Foundations for a Global Theology.* Maryknoll, N.Y.: Orbis Books, 1991.

Moltmann, Jürgen. *The Spirit of Life: A Universal Affirmation.* Trans. Margaret Kohl. Minneapolis: Fortress Press, 1992.

Ricoeur, Paul. "Religion, Atheism, and Faith." In Alasdair MacIntyre and Paul Ricoeur, *The Religious Significance of Atheism,* pp.59–98. New York: Columbia University Press, 1969.

Royce, Josiah. *The Problem of Christianity.* Intro. John E. Smith. Chicago: University of Chicago Press, 1968.

Smith, Steven G. *The Concept of the Spiritual: An Essay in First Philosophy.* Philadelphia: Temple University Press, 1988.

*Stendahl, Krister. *Energy for Life: Reflections on the Theme "Come, Holy Spirit—Renew the Whole Creation."* Geneva, Switzerland: WCC Publications, 1990.

Tillich, Paul. *Christianity and the Encounter of the World Religions.* New York: Columbia University Press, 1963.

_____. *The Future of Religions.* Ed. Jerald C. Brauer. New York: Harper and Row, 1966.

_____. *Systematic Theology.* Vol. 3: Life and the Spirit, History and the Kingdom of God. Chicago: University of Chicago Press, 1963.

Welker, Michael. *God the Spirit.* Trans. John F. Hoffmeyer. Minneapolis: Fortress Press, 1994.

Index

181